# SIMPLY DELECTABLE

## SHARON GLASS

Graphic Arts Center Publishing®

www.sharonrecipes.com

Published in the United States of America by
Graphic Arts Center Publishing®
An imprint of Graphic Arts Center Publishing Company
P.O. Box 10306, Portland, Oregon 97296-0306
www.gacpc.com

President: Charles M. Hopkins
Associate Publisher: Douglas A. Pfeiffer
Editorial Staff: Timothy W. Frew, Tricia Brown, Jean Andrews, Kathy Matthews,
  Jean Bond-Slaughter
Production Staff: Richard L. Owsiany, Joanna Goebel

Photographer: Janyon Boshoff
Food stylist: Christelle Weber
Design and layout: Patricia Braune
Production Manager: Toni Venturini
Props: Congo Joe and Loads of Linen
Reproduction: Tone Graphics

While every effort has been made to ensure the accuracy of the facts and data contained in this publi-
cation, no responsibility can be accepted by the author for errors and omissions or their consequences.

Library of Congress Cataloging-in-Publication Data
Glass, Sharon.
  [Simply delicious]
  Simply delectable / Sharon Glass.
    p. cm.
  Originally published: Simply delicious. Cape Town : Creative Pub., 2000.
  Includes index.
  ISBN 1-55868-690-8 (sb)
    1. Cookery. I. Title.

TX714 .G594 2002
641.5—dc21

                                    2002024482

Printed in Hong Kong

# FOREWORD

This book is for all of you who adore the best things in life—good food using the best ingredients, the freshest fruits and vegetables and creating taste sensations for all your family and friends.

I love cooking.

I get no greater pleasure than from sharing these wonderful concoctions with you.

I'm sure that you will be inspired to cook up a storm.

# THANKS

This book would not have been possible without the loving support and backup of my wonderful husband, Anthony.

Thanks must go to my mother, Norma, whose love of cooking inspired me from my early childhood.

Thanks to my children, Teri, Ricci and Jake (my official fan club), who have had to live with a busy mom in a busy kitchen constantly tasting and cooking over the years.

The honest objectivity and praise of all my family each and every Friday night (and so many other nights) have made these recipes what they are—your unstinting belief in me over the years has been a pillar of strength.

My family in America who have been my "behind-the-scenes" support system, and who never stopped encouraging me.

The unofficial tasters in my kitchen, who must wash dishes in their sleep, have also added to this collection.

My students and friends for their ongoing support.

Credit has to be given to the people who made this book into what it is today—from these unbelievable photographs by Janyon, to the simple yet stunning styling of the food by Christelle, to the hours and hours of layout and proofing that was required by Patricia.

# CONTENTS

Red pepper & feta pies

RED PEPPER & FETA PIES

CHICKEN SATAY

# HORS D'OEUVRES

LAYER SMOKED SALMON PÂTÉ

SPANAKOPITA TART

The word "hors d'oeuvres" sounds so fancy, but simple first courses that are not too starchy are a marvelous preface to your meal.

We all lead such busy lives that no one has time to prepare involved hors d'oeuvres. I really don't believe in filling your guests up with too many starters or they won't eat the main course.

The hors d'oeuvres that I have chosen provide a variety of tantalizing tastes and display a mixture of vegetarian as well as meat, chicken and fish choices.

I love using phyllo pastry because it is so versatile, easy-to-use and light, hence the numerous recipes. Its real advantage is the fact that it can be prepared ahead and refrigerated.

When using foil, like in the Mediterranean Crèpe Stack, I always place food against the dull side of the foil or have the dull side facing outward into the oven. This way, there is no reflection in the oven.

# HORS D'OEUVRES

CHICKEN SATAY

DELICIOUS FOCACCIA

FRESH ASPARAGUS & MUSHROOM PIZZA

LAYERED SMOKED SALMON PÂTÉ

MARINATED SMOKED SALMON CARPACCIO

MEDITERRANEAN CRÈPE STACK

MEXICAN SALMON TORTILLA DELIGHT

PISSALADIÈRE

RED PEPPER & FETA PIES

SPANAKOPITA TART

THAI FISH CAKES WITH SWEET CHILI SAUCE

## CHICKEN SATAY

What a nice appetizer to serve with drinks! They can be skewered the day before your function and brushed with the sauce a few hours before and then grilled. You can serve them at room temperature and sprinkle with some cilantro leaves before serving.

1 tsp (5ml) minced garlic

2 tsps (10ml) freshly chopped cilantro

½ tsp (2.5ml) medium curry powder

½ to 1 tsp (2.5-5ml) chili paste

1 tsp (5ml) finely chopped fresh ginger or
  ½ tsp (2.5ml) dry ground ginger

2 Tbs (30ml) soft brown sugar

2 tsps (10ml) lemon juice

2 Tbs (30ml) smooth peanut butter

½ cup (125ml) coconut milk

½ tsp (2.5ml) red curry paste

4 boneless and skinless chicken breasts,
  cut into very thin strips and threaded on
  bamboo skewers that have been soaked
  in water for a few minutes

Mix all sauce ingredients together. Bring to a boil and allow to thicken slightly.

Thread chicken on skewers (zigzag style) through pointed side, using only 2 strips per skewer.

Place skewers on a baking sheet lined with foil and sprayed with nonstick cooking spray. Brush one side of chicken with basting sauce. Face pieces with chicken inwards and cover open sticks with foil to avoid them burning.

Preheat grill. Place directly under grill. Grill for 5 mins. Turn and brush other side with sauce and grill another 5 mins. Do not allow to dry out.

Baste with remaining sauce just before serving.

Serve at room temperature. Decorate with fresh cilantro.

MAKES 8–10 SKEWERS

## DELICIOUS FOCACCIA

3 Tbs (15g) instant dry yeast

1 cup (250g) cake flour

1 cup (250g) semolina

12 Tbs (180ml) olive oil, divided

1½ Tbs (22.5ml) sugar

1¼ cup (300ml) lukewarm water

1 tsp (5ml) salt

Mix yeast, flour, semolina and sugar together. Stir well. Add 6 Tbs (90ml) olive oil. Then add the lukewarm water and the salt. Mix together to make a dough.

Remove from bowl and knead until very smooth. Add a little extra flour if necessary. When smooth, cover with damp cloth and allow to rise until double in size. Then pat out into a rectangular shape about ½ inch (1.5 cm) thick.

Drizzle remaining olive oil over your hands and poke holes into the focaccia with your fingers.

If desired, place a few unpeeled garlic cloves all over, some fresh rosemary, salt, pepper and sun-dried tomatoes. Allow to rise again.

Bake in 425 F (220 C) oven for 15 to 20 mins or until golden.

## FRESH ASPARAGUS & MUSHROOM PIZZA

The dough is crispy, the feta is salty and the stunning green color of the asparagus makes this a perfect starter.

### DOUGH

1½ cups (375ml) cake flour

1½ Tbs (7.5g) instant yeast

½ tsp (2.5ml) salt

1 Tbs (15ml) sugar

¾ cup (175ml) warm water

1 Tbs (15ml) honey

2 tsps (10ml) oil

For Dough: Mix all dry ingredients together in a bowl. Stir water, honey and oil together. Add to dry ingredients. Mix together to form a dough and continue to knead on a floured surface for a few minutes or until dough is smooth and elastic.

Place dough in a well-oiled bowl. Cover with plastic wrap and then a kitchen towel. Set aside in a warm place and allow to rise until bubbling and spongy for approx. 1 hour.

Roll out to fit pizza baking tray (10 inch or 26cm). Preheat oven to 400 F (200 C).

## TOPPING

½ cup (125ml) canned chopped tomato

8 oz (250g) white mushrooms, sliced, sautéed and seasoned

8 oz (250g) fresh asparagus spears

1½ cups (375ml) mozzarella cheese

½ cup (125ml) crumbled feta cheese

Spread with the toppings: First spread the chopped tomato and season with salt, pepper and oregano. Sprinkle with cheeses. Then scatter mushrooms and arrange asparagus in spokes from center outward. Season again and sprinkle with more dry oregano.

Bake 400 F (200 C) for 20 mins or until golden.

SERVES: 10–12

Delicious focaccia

Fresh asparagus and mushroom pizza

## LAYERED SMOKED SALMON PÂTÉ

Your guests will *ooh* and *aah* over this very rich, no calories barred starter. Serve with some fresh Italian bread or a warm focaccia.

3 Tbs (45ml) freshly chopped chives
1 lb (500g) smooth cream cheese
1 lb (500g) smoked salmon
1 small red onion, thinly sliced
3 Tbs (45ml) capers, drained
Freshly ground black pepper
2 or 3 avocados, coarsely mashed and mixed
  with lemon juice
1 small loaf tin lined with plastic wrap

Line a loaf tin with plastic wrap. Spread in thin layers: smoked salmon, cream cheese, chives, salmon, avocado, black pepper, capers, onions, smoked salmon, cream cheese, chives, black pepper, capers, onions, avocado, smoked salmon.

Place a sheet of plastic wrap on top of salmon and press down lightly with your hand to compact it.

Place in fridge for at least 3 hours to set.

TO SERVE: Remove top layer of plastic wrap. Invert on to a plate and remove other plastic wrap. You require a very sharp serrated knife dipped in hot water to cut the pâté.

TIP: PLACE WHOLE UNPEELED AVOCADO IN BOILING WATER FOR 1 MIN. PEEL. THE AVOCADO WILL NOT GO BLACK. THIS CAN BE DONE A FEW HOURS AHEAD.

SERVES: 4–6

## MARINATED SMOKED SALMON CARPACCIO

I love making this because it's so easy to prepare, and so exquisitely beautiful in its simplicity. Served with some fresh rye or Italian rolls, it makes an elegant starter.

1 lb (500g) smoked salmon
2-3 Tbs (30-45ml) light olive oil
2-3 Tbs (30-45ml) fresh lemon juice
4 Tbs (60ml) freshly chopped chives
Freshly ground black pepper

Roll each piece of salmon loosely. Arrange in circles on a platter in a single layer. Drizzle with a little olive oil. Sprinkle with chives and lots of freshly ground black pepper. This can be done a few hours ahead.

Half an hour before serving drizzle with lemon juice.

SERVES: 3–4

## MEDITERRANEAN CRÈPE STACK

If you want to impress your guests, serve this, which suits all tastes and can be prepared ahead of time. Bake just before serving

### CRÈPES

1 cup (250ml) cake flour
2 jumbo eggs
1½ cups (310ml) lowfat milk
1 tsp (5ml) mustard powder
2 Tbs (30ml) melted salted butter
1 Tbs (15ml) brandy

Make a well in center of flour. Place eggs in well. Whisk in milk, and lastly mustard, butter and brandy.

Heat a medium nonstick frying pan. Spray with nonstick spray and heat on high until very hot. Ladle a little mixture into frying pan and turn once until just done on each side.

Place cooked crèpes between sheets of wax (greaseproof) paper until ready to use. Makes 9 crèpes.

## FILLING

1 cup (250ml) crumbled feta

1 cup (250ml) coarsely grated cheddar

9½ oz (300g) spinach, finely shredded and
   wilted, seasoned with salt and pepper

½ bunch spring onions, sliced thinly

½ cup (125ml) smooth lowfat cottage cheese

8 oz (250g) grated mozzarella

1 lb (500g) mushrooms, sliced and sautéed
   until dry

Preheat oven to 350 F (160 C).

Spray a quiche or pie dish with nonstick spray.

Place 1 crèpe in dish and layer fillings on top
alternating with crèpes –
Layers 1 & 4 - spinach
Layers 2 & 5 - feta and cheddar
Layers 3 & 6 - mushrooms
Layer 7       - cream cheese
Layer 8       - cheddar and feta
Top           - grated mozzarella and parmesan

Cover with foil, dull side out. Spray shiny side of
foil to prevent sticking. Bake covered for 30 mins.
Then uncover and continue to bake for another
20 mins.

SERVES: 10–12

# MEXICAN SALMON TORTILLA DELIGHT

I love this different starter because it looks wonderful on a platter and becomes a conversation piece.

9½ oz (300g) tricolor very thin pasta,
   cooked 'al dente'

3 Tbs (45ml) olive oil

Boil each color pasta separately until just cooked
through. Rinse with cold water. Toss with drop of
olive oil and keep separate in 3 small bowls.

1¼ oz (35g) packet taco seasoning

1 cup (250ml) sour cream or yogurt

1 cup (250ml) mayonnaise

Mix taco seasoning with sour cream and
mayonnaise in a bowl. Set aside.

14 oz (400g) plain tortilla chips

1 avocado, sliced

8 oz (250g) smoked salmon,
   cut into thin strips

1 cup (250ml) mild salsa

2 scallions, very finely chopped

2 Tbs (30ml) very finely chopped parsley

One hour before serving, mix each pasta with a
little taco sauce.

Using a large, flat platter, spoon a little salsa in
3 sections on the base of platter. Then top each
mound with different color pasta mixture. You will
have three fat rows, leaving a border around the
edge of the platter. Decorate with smoked salmon
in between the rows of pasta and place avocado in
between salmon pieces. Sprinkle with scallions and
chopped parsley.

Just before serving, sprinkle lightly crushed tortilla
chips around edge of entire platter.

Can be refrigerated an hour or two ahead of time
without the tortilla chips.

SERVES: 10–12

## PISSALADIÈRE

A typically French pizza without the tomato. It makes an absolutely delicious snack to serve with drinks before a meal. The caramelized onions are sweet and golden.

### DOUGH

1 tsp (5ml) instant dry yeast
2 tsps (10ml) sugar
½ tsp (2.5ml) salt
2 cups (500ml) cake flour
¾ cups (175ml) warm water
1 Tbs (15ml) olive oil

Stir dry ingredients together. Mix moist ingredients together and add to dry ingredients. Knead to form a dough and continue to knead until dough is very smooth. Place in a lightly oiled dish. Cover with plastic wrap and allow to rise for at least 1 hour. Dough must be spongelike. When ready to use, roll out into a rectangle on a small sprayed baking tray.

### TOPPING

2 Tbs (15g) salted butter
5 Tbs (75ml) olive oil
10 scallions, thinly sliced
4 dry bay leaves
2 Tbs (30ml) sugar
2 tsps (10ml) salt
2 Tbs (30ml) dry white wine
Black olives
Anchovies
Grated parmesan or feta

In a large frying pan, melt butter with oil over low heat. Add half the onions and 2 bay leaves. Sprinkle with 1 Tbs of sugar and half the salt. Top with remaining onions, bay leaves, sugar and salt. Cover and allow to cook for 20 mins.

Uncover. Then increase heat to medium and cook until golden, stirring occasionally. Add wine and bring to a boil, scraping up any browned bits. Onions must be golden when finished cooking.

Spread topping over rolled out dough. Dot with olives, anchovies and grated parmesan or feta if desired. Cut off excess dough.

Preheat oven to 400 F (200 C). Bake on middle rack of oven for 15 mins or until golden.

SERVES: 8–10

## RED PEPPER & FETA PIES

These freeze very well and are absolutely scrumptious. Allow 2 or 3 per person, because they'll want more and more!

6 to 8 sheets phyllo
Melted butter for brushing
2 large red peppers, seeded and chopped very fine
2 Tbs (30ml) olive oil
1⅓ cup (330ml) herb or plain feta cheese
Black pepper

Sauté red peppers in olive oil in a frying pan on medium heat until softened. Allow mixture to cool. Then place feta and red pepper mixture in food processor and add black pepper. Process until mixture is smooth. Set aside.

Brush phyllo with melted butter one sheet at a time. Cut each sheet into 4 squares. Spread very little mixture along one side of the brushed phyllo and then roll up like a sausage. Twist into a spiral and fasten the outer end with a toothpick.

Continue making more spirals until all filling is finished.

Place all spirals on baking paper on a baking sheet and brush with additional melted butter and sprinkle with sesame or poppy seeds if desired. Preheat oven to 375 F (180 C) and bake uncovered in middle of oven until golden—about 20 mins. Remove toothpicks when spirals are baked.

NOTE: Unbaked phyllo pies can be left covered with plastic wrap in fridge for a few hours before baking or frozen in an airtight container unbaked.

MAKES 32 SPIRALS

Mexican salmon tortilla delight

Layered smoked salmon pâté

Mediterranean crèpe stack

## SPANAKOPITA TART

The pine nuts give this tart a different touch and it is easy to cut because of its shape.

½ cup (125ml) pine nuts
2 Tbs (30ml) olive oil
9½ oz (300g) fresh spinach, spine removed
  and very finely shredded
1 cup (250ml) crumbled feta with herbs
Salt and pepper
¼ cup (60ml) grated parmesan
5 sheets phyllo brushed with butter

Preheat oven to 375 F (180 C).

Toast pine nuts on a baking sheet for 10 mins at 300 F (140 C).

Quickly cook spinach in olive oil in a large frying pan, seasoning as you cook with salt and pepper, until spinach is just wilted.

Place feta in food processor and process until finely crumbled. Then add spinach, salt and pepper and pulse just to mix in. Remove from food processor and stir in pine nuts. Add a little parmesan (if desired).

Brush each of 5 sheets phyllo with melted butter, and stack 1 on top of the other. Place phyllo stack on a baking sheet. Spread filling in center leaving a border around edges. Then fold in the edges to make a square base with sides. Brush edges with butter. Sprinkle filling with remaining parmesan. Place toothpicks on each corner to prevent phyllo from unrolling.

Bake for 20 mins in middle of oven or until golden.

NOTE: To make ahead of time, cover entire tart with plastic wrap and place covered in fridge until ready to bake.

SERVES: 6–8

## THAI FISH CAKES WITH SWEET CHILI SAUCE

These fish cakes are simply delicious and so easy to make. They make a nice change from the usual fish cake, and the sauce gives the final touch.

1 lb (500g) minced hake or cod or other
  firm white fish
4¾ oz (150g) blanched green beans,
  cut into pieces
¼ cup (60ml) red pepper
Handful of cilantro
½ tsp (2.5ml) chili paste
1 Tbs (15ml) lime juice or bottled lemon
  juice
1 tsp (5ml) salt
1 tsp (5ml) paprika
1 Tbs (15ml) sweet soy sauce
1 scallion, cut into pieces
Black pepper
1 egg

Breadcrumbs for dipping

Place all ingredients in food processor and process until quite smooth. Mound mixture into ovals the size of a dessert spoon and dip lightly in crumbs just to coat fish.

Sauté on medium high heat in approx. ½ inch (1 cm) of sunflower oil until golden brown. Drain on paper towel.

### SWEET & SOUR SAUCE
½ cup (125ml) sugar
¼ cup (60ml) water
⅓ cup (80ml) white wine vinegar
½ tsp (2.5ml) salt
2 Tbs (30ml) finely chopped cilantro leaves
½ tsp (2.5ml) chili paste or chopped chilis
  or red pepper

Place all ingredients in a small pot and heat gently just to dissolve the sugar.

SERVES: 4–6

Spanakopita tart

Roasted cherry tomato soup

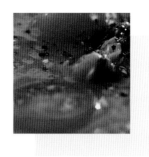

ROASTED CHERRY TOMATO SOUP

COUNTRY MINESTRONE SOUP

# SOUPS

PUMPKIN SOUP

SPLIT PEA SOUP

We always think of soup as being a heavy, hearty winter dish. But it has been transformed through the use of different ingredients and methods into fresh, light and satisfying dishes.

All soups are very easy to make and can be made ahead of time and frozen. If you are freezing the soup, freeze without the cream, and only add the cream when reheating. I like to use Knorr cubes as I think they have more flavor than the others, but if you are kosher and use Telma cubes or powder, then I have given you the correct quantities. Remember that Telma Chicken cubes are Parev and should be used in place of vegetable cubes, which will thicken your soup because of the potato in them. Should you not wish to use any cubes because of the MSG, then you need to buy Plantaforce or other natural vegetable bouillon cubes from a health shop as well as the seasoning salt Herbamare.

Where I have said "vegetable stock" or "chicken stock," that means whatever cubes I have specified dissolved in that number of cups of boiling water.

I love to serve my soups with some lightly grilled Italian toasts like croutons. Lightly brush some Italian bread or rolls with some herbed olive oil, by adding some mixed dry herbs like basil, rosemary and oregano into the olive oil and grill for 2 minutes on the bread side until lightly golden and toasted. Alternatively, you can make some fresh herb oils using coriander, basil, rosemary and thyme.

Another great idea is to make my delicious focaccia to serve with your soups (refer to Hors d'oeuvres).

# SOUPS

COUNTRY MINESTRONE SOUP

CREAM OF LEEK SOUP

CREAM OF ROASTED VEGETABLE SOUP

CREAM OF SWEETCORN SOUP

EGGPLANT SOUP

ITALIAN BEAN SOUP

JAPANESE CHICKEN NOODLE & VEGETABLE SOUP

MUSHROOM CAPPUCCINO SOUP

PUMPKIN SOUP

ROASTED CHERRY TOMATO SOUP

ROASTED PUMPKIN & RED ONION SOUP

SPLIT PEA SOUP

SWEET POTATO AND GINGER SOUP

## COUNTRY MINESTRONE SOUP

You'll make this soup a million times because everyone loves it. It makes a huge amount and you will need to add water or stock to it because it is very thick. If there are "ready cut" fresh vegetables available, and they are cut in small cubes, then take the opportunity and use them, they will make your life much easier.

2 onions, finely diced
3 large carrots, chopped coarsely
3 sticks celery, chopped coarsely
3 potatoes, chopped coarsely
4 baby zucchini, chopped in small chunks
7 oz (200g) green beans,
  cut into small pieces
A few spinach leaves, finely shredded
½ butternut, cut into small chunks
¼ cup (60ml) olive oil
2 Tbs (30ml) butter or margarine
12 cups (3 Litres) chicken or vegetable stock
  (5 Knorr or 8 Telma cubes)
2 28-oz cans (2 x 410g tins) whole peeled
  tomatoes, chopped with liquid
½ cup (125ml) tomato purée

Heat oil and butter or margarine in a large pot. Add onions and cook over medium heat until golden. Add carrots and celery and cook for a few minutes stirring occasionally. (This brings out the flavor.)

Add the remaining vegetables and sauté lightly for a few minutes. Lastly add stock, canned tomatoes and tomato purée. Bring to a boil and then lower heat and allow to simmer for at least 2 to 3 hours, or until soup is thick. Add additional water if necessary.

Mash some of the vegetables to thicken soup.

NOTE: Freezes very well.

SERVES: 15–20

## CREAM OF LEEK SOUP

If you love vichysoisse, then this is even nicer without all the potatoes. It is an elegant soup and milk can be substituted for the cream to make it less fattening.

4 Tbs (60ml) butter or margarine
8 - 10 large leeks, sliced (white only)
3 medium to large potatoes, cut into chunks
2 Tbs (30ml) flour
8 cups (2 Litres) chicken stock
  (3 Knorr or 6 Telma Cubes)
½ cup (125ml) cream or milk (optional)
Chopped chives for decorating

Sauté leeks in butter or margarine until softened.

Stir in flour and cook for 1 min. Add stock and potatoes and allow to simmer for at least 1 hour or until potatoes are soft.

Purée entire mixture. Return to pot and reheat gently.

Only add cream or milk when reheating. Season to taste. Serve with chopped chives.

NOTE: Can be frozen without the cream.

SERVES: 8–10

Country minestrone soup

# CREAM OF ROASTED VEGETABLE SOUP

This soup is not your average vegetable soup. The grilled vegetables change the flavor and make it a much more elegant and creamy soup.

3 Tbs (45ml) olive oil
1 tsp (5ml) minced garlic
1 large eggplant, peeled and cubed
8 oz (250g) summer squash, quartered
8 medium baby zucchini, sliced
1 red pepper, sliced
3 Tbs (45ml) chopped onion
2 Tbs (30ml) butter or margarine
2½ Tbs (37ml) flour
8 cups (2 Litres) chicken or vegetable stock
  (4 Knorr or 6 Telma cubes)

Preheat oven to 200 C (400 F).

Heat olive oil in a pot and sauté garlic lightly for a few minutes. Add vegetables and season with salt and pepper. Sauté for a few minutes.
Then place in a roasting pan and roast uncovered on middle rack of oven for 30 to 40 mins or until nicely browned.

In the same pot, while the vegs are roasting, melt butter or margarine and stir in flour. Cook for 1 minute. Then add stock and whisk while allowing it to thicken. Cook for 5 mins.

When vegetables are cooked, purée them with the stock until smooth. If soup is too thick, add more stock. Adjust seasoning.

NOTES: Can be frozen.

SERVES: 8–10

# CREAM OF SWEETCORN SOUP

You'll enjoy the subtle sweetness that comes through from the two types of corn. This soup is very quick and easy to make.

4 ears of corn, cooked and cut from cob
3 3½-oz (3 x 100g) packets fresh baby corn
  or 2 14-oz cans (2 x 410g tins) drained
  baby corn, cut into pieces
2 Tbs (30ml) butter or margarine
3 large carrots
½ onion
6 cups (1½ Litres) vegetable stock
  (4 Knorr or 6 Telma cubes)
½ cup (125ml) cream
Black pepper
Chopped parsley

Chop onion and carrot together in food processor until very fine. Sauté in butter or margarine until softened. Add baby corn and cook for a few minutes. Then add stock and corn.

Allow to cook for 15 minutes. Remove from stove and purée. Strain through a coarse strainer. Place ¾ of pulp back into the soup; otherwise the soup will be very thin.

Stir in cream and black pepper. Sprinkle with chopped parsley just before serving.

SERVES: 6–8

# EGGPLANT SOUP

Don't tell them what kind of soup it is. My family doesn't eat eggplant but they raved about this soup, because it tastes like vichysoisse. It is also one of the easiest soups to make.

3 Tbs (45ml) olive oil
6 leeks, whites only, sliced
2 lb (1kg) eggplant,
  peeled and cut into pieces
8 cups (2 Litres) vegetable or chicken stock
  (4 Knorr or 5 Telma cubes)
½ cup (125ml) cream (optional)

Sauté leeks in olive oil until softened. Add eggplant and stock and simmer until softened—about 20 mins. Purée. Add ½ cup cream if desired. The soup freezes extremely well with or without cream.

SERVES: 6–8

Cream of sweetcorn soup

## ITALIAN BEAN SOUP

A hearty vegetable soup especially for vegetarians, and the olive oil gives it a subtle Italian flavor.

½ cup (125ml) pearl barley

4 baby zucchinis, diced

8 oz (250g) spinach, shredded

2 potatoes, diced

1 small butternut, diced

2 onions, diced

3 carrots, diced

2 sticks celery, diced

14 oz (410g) canned cannellini beans,
  drained

4 oz (125g) thin green beans, sliced thinly

½ cup (125ml) fresh or frozen peas

2 Tbs (30ml) olive oil

2 Tbs (30ml) salt

2 Tbs (30ml) fresh basil

Cover barley with water and simmer for 45 mins until soft. Drain. Do not allow to get mushy.

Place baby zucchinis, spinach, potatoes, butternut, onion, carrots and celery into a pot and cover with at least 6 cups cold water. Add 2 Tbs salt and bring to a boil. Add black pepper and boil for 15 mins or until softened. Remove half the vegetables and purée. Return them to the pot.

Simmer the beans and peas in salted water for about 10 mins or until softened. Reserve the water.

Add the beans, peas, barley and olive oil to the rest of the vegetables. Simmer gently, stirring from time to time.

If the soup is too thick, add some of the reserved salted water.

Just before serving, stir in some finely chopped basil.

SERVES: 6–8

## JAPANESE CHICKEN NOODLE & VEGETABLE SOUP

When you need a colorful, lowfat soup that takes two minutes to make—this is the one.

2 boneless and skinless breasts

6 cups (1.5 Litres) chicken stock
  (3 Knorr or 5 Telma cubes)

1 carrot, sliced

4 oz (125ml) mushrooms, sliced

14 oz (410g) canned baby corn spears,
  cut in half lengthwise

1 tsp (5ml) sesame oil

1 piece ginger, cut into pieces

Handful fresh parsley

3 spinach or tah tsai leaves*, finely shredded

2 scallions, very thinly sliced

2 Tbs (30ml) yellow miso paste (optional)

4 oz (125g) very thin egg noodles or
  Japanese Udon noodles

Boil breasts in water, adding stock, carrot, mushrooms, corn spears, sesame oil, ginger and parsley. Bring to a boil and then reduce heat and simmer with lid on for 20 to 25 mins or until vegetables are softened.

Remove ginger pieces and parsley and stir in miso paste to dissolve. If not using miso, taste for seasoning and adjust with extra stock to make a rich soup.

Shred some of the chicken into very thin strips and place back in broth.

Lastly add spinach and scallions.

Boil noodles and place in bowls before adding soup. Sprinkle with a few cilantro leaves before serving.

NOTE: Udon noodles do not need to be cooked.

* see substitutes

Japanese chicken noodle & vegetable soup

## MUSHROOM CAPPUCCINO SOUP

The creaminess of the mushrooms are enhanced by the rosemary and sherry to make the soup rich and delicious.

2 Tbs (30ml) olive oil
1 Tbs (15ml) butter or margarine
1 onion, chopped
2 leeks, sliced
1 Tbs (15ml) fresh rosemary
1 lb (500g) medium brown mushrooms, sliced
8 oz (250g) white mushrooms, sliced
¼ cup (60ml) flour
3 cups (750ml) chicken or vegetable stock (3 Knorr or 4 Telma cubes)
Salt and pepper
1 cup (250ml) lowfat milk
1 Tbs (15ml) soy sauce
Pinch of sugar
2 Tbs (30ml) medium cream sherry
¼ cup (60ml) cream (optional)
Milk for froth on top

Heat oil and butter. Add onion and leeks and allow to soften. Do not brown. Add rosemary and brown mushrooms. Sauté until softened. Then add flour. Cook for 1 min. Then add stock allowing it to thicken. Season with salt and pepper.

Place lid on pot and allow to simmer for 15 mins. Purée until smooth. Place back in pot. Add remaining button mushrooms, milk, soy sauce and sugar. Adjust seasoning.

Simmer for 10 mins. Then stir in sherry and drizzle in cream. Add chopped parsley just before serving.

Using a milk frother, froth some milk. Pour soup into cups. Place a little foam on top of each cup just before serving.

## PUMPKIN SOUP

Delicious, creamy and hearty, this makes a large pot of soup and will be loved by everyone (including the kids).

2 Tbs (30ml) butter or margarine
1 onion, coarsely chopped
2 potatoes, coarsely chopped
4 large carrots, peeled and sliced thickly
2 lbs (1 kg) pumpkin (either fresh or frozen)
6 cups (1.5 Litres) chicken or vegetable stock (4 Knorr or 6 Telma cubes)
1 tsp (5ml) salt
1 Tbs (15ml) sugar or
    1½ Tbs artificial sweetener
½ cup (125ml) cream (optional)

Sauté onion in butter or margarine in a large pot on high heat until golden. Add potatoes and carrots and sauté for a few minutes. Add pumpkin and stock and allow to simmer with lid on for at least 1 to 2 hours or until vegetables are soft.

Purée until smooth. Add more water if too thick. Add sugar and salt to taste. (Should have a slightly salty, sweet taste.)

If adding cream, add only after reheating on low heat.

NOTE: Can be frozen without the cream.

SERVES: 6–8

## ROASTED CHERRY TOMATO SOUP

Served hot or cold, this is a modern gazpacho. The cherry tomatoes give it a very sweet flavor.

14 oz (400g) yellow cherry tomatoes, unpeeled (if available)*
28 oz (800g) red cherry tomatoes, unpeeled
3 bay leaves
2 Tbs (30ml) marjoram
3 shallots or red onions, cut into pieces (or 6 scallions, sliced)
¼ cup (60ml) olive oil
Freshly ground black pepper
Salt
¼ cup (60ml) sugar
4 cups (1 Litre) vegetable stock (4 Knorr or 6 - 8 Telma cubes)
1 cup (2 x 125ml) sun-dried tomato pesto
1 tsps (5ml) Herbamare or other natural herb seasoning salt
⅓ cup (80ml) cream
Croutons for serving

Preheat oven to 350 F (160 C).

Place cherry tomatoes in a roasting pan. Sprinkle with salt and pepper. Add onions or shallots, marjoram, bay leaves and sugar.

Place on middle rack of oven and roast for 1 hour or until softened. Remove from roasting pan and place in a mixing bowl.

Purée tomatoes. Place in a large pot and add stock and water. Heat until just warmed through. Add sun-dried tomato pesto and adjust seasoning. Add cream if desired. Cool slightly. Serve with croutons.

HANDY TIP: Strain soup and then place some pulp back into the soup to thicken it.

SERVES: 8–10

* increase quantity of red cherry tomatoes if yellow are unavailable

## ROASTED PUMPKIN & RED ONION SOUP

If you like pumpkin soup with a Thai flavor, then this is a little different. It has just the right amount of spice to add zest to your taste buds.

⅓ cup (80ml) olive oil
4 lbs (2 kg) pumpkin chunks
2 Tbs (30ml) finely chopped ginger
2 red onions, cut into pieces
1 cup (250ml) coconut milk
1 Tbs (15ml) red curry paste
2-3 Tbs (30-45ml) finely chopped cilantro
6 cups (750ml) chicken or vegetable stock (4 Knorr or 6 Telma cubes)

Preheat oven to 400 F (200 C). Place pumpkin pieces in a roasting pan. Add ginger. Drizzle with ¾ of olive oil. Place on middle rack of oven and roast until brown. Turn over and roast other side (until pumpkin is soft). Set aside.

Place red onion in same roasting pan. Drizzle with remaining olive oil. Roast for 20 mins or until soft. Watch carefully, turning them, as they will burn.

Place onion and pumpkin in a food processor. Process until quite smooth. Add some of the stock to thin out the mixture slightly.

In a large pot sauté red curry paste and cilantro in 2 Tbs (30ml) oil for 2 mins. Add coconut milk and remaining stock and heat gently. Stir in processed pumpkin and onion mixture. Place lid on pot and heat through.

NOTE: Can be made a few days ahead and refrigerated. When reheating, do not heat on a very high heat.

SERVES: 8–10

## SPLIT PEA SOUP

When you need a hearty, thick soup, this one will do just the trick, and it doesn't have any meat in it. An all-time favorite of mine, I'm sure it will become one of yours. You can add some beef shin to give it more flavor. Remove the meat before puréeing.

1 lb (500g) yellow split peas
16 cups (4 Litres) chicken or vegetable stock
  (6 Knorr or 8 Telma cubes)
2 celery sticks with leaves, cut into pieces
2 medium carrots, diced
1 large onion, diced
1 large turnip, peeled and quartered
Freshly ground pepper

In a large pot, bring the split peas and stock to boil. Turn heat to medium-low and simmer for 45 minutes. Add all remaining ingredients to the pot and gently boil until all vegetables are tender.

Purée soup in food processor or blender. Add additional stock if necessary for flavor.

NOTE: Can be frozen.

SERVES: 12–15

## SWEET POTATO AND GINGER SOUP

This is such a different soup with a gentle sweetness from the sweet potato; a little ginger enhances it, and the salsa and cilantro oil add the finishing touch.

3 Tbs (45ml) olive oil
2 Tbs (30ml) grated orange peel and juice
1 tsp (5ml) curry powder (medium)
¾ handful cilantro
1 tsp (5ml) sugar
1 Tbs (15ml) grated ginger
2 lbs (1kg) sweet potato, cut into chunks

4 parsnips, peeled and cut into pieces
4-5 leeks, sliced
4 carrots, cut into pieces
2 tsps (10ml) salt
4 cups (1 Litre) vegetable stock
  (3 Knorr or 4 Telma cubes)
2 cups (500ml) lowfat milk
½ cup (125ml) light cream (if desired)

Heat olive oil and add orange peel and juice, curry powder, cilantro, sugar, grated ginger and sweet potato. Sauté everything for about 5 minutes until browned and slightly softened. Add parsnips, leeks and carrots, and sauté for another 5 mins.

Add vegetable stock and simmer for about 30 mins or until vegetables are soft. Purée entire mixture. Add milk. Then add cream (if desired). Adjust seasoning.

Serve with a spoonful of tomato/pepper salsa and a drizzle of cilantro oil.

### CILANTRO OIL

1 oz (30g) cilantro
2 tsps (10ml) coarse salt
3 Tbs (45ml) white wine vinegar
¾ cup (175ml) olive oil

Blanch cilantro for 1 min. Place cilantro, coarse salt and white wine vinegar in food processor. Process until mixed through. Pour olive oil through feed tube and continue to process until you have a liquid.

### TOMATO/PEPPER SALSA

2 tomatoes, seeded and chopped
1 yellow pepper, chopped
Salt and pepper
1 Tbs (15ml) fresh cilantro, chopped

Mix all ingredients together.
Drizzle soup with cilantro oil and place a drop of salsa in the center of the bowl.

SERVES: 8–10

Roasted pumpkin and red onion soup

Mushroom cappuccino soup

Sweet potato and ginger soup

Seared salmon caesar salad

ROASTED MUSHROOM SALAD

CREAMY SPINACH SALAD

# SALADS

CONFETTI SALAD

SLOW ROASTED BEET SALAD

Salads are everybody's favorite. There is nothing nicer than a cold, freshly tossed salad.

You will love these because not only are they delicious, but the different ingredients, with their myriad of colors, create a vivid picture.

Most of my dressings can be made well ahead of time and refrigerated.

In all of my salads I use light olive oil, because otherwise the dressings are too strong and can alter the taste of the salad.

Never overdress your salads as they go soggy. The dressings are enhanced by the use of salt. I always use coarse salt grinders, as well as fresh pepper grinders. Do not use too much vinegar; otherwise the dressing becomes too strong.

Blanching of vegetables is essential in salads because some vegetables should not be served raw. To blanch them, you bring a pot of water to a boil. Add some salt and then place your vegetables in the boiling water for a few minutes (each recipe indicates cooking times). Plunge vegetables immediately into ice water to stop them from cooking further. Dry them very well. This can all be done the day before you need them. Keep refrigerated in a sealed container.

# SALADS

CAESAR SALAD

CONFETTI SALAD

CREAMY SPINACH SALMON SALAD

FRESH GRILLED SALMON SALAD

GREEN BEAN, LEEK & POTATO SALAD

GRILLED CORN SALAD

GRILLED VEGETABLE SALAD

PASTA & ROASTED VEGETABLE SALAD

ROASTED MUSHROOM SALAD WITH PINE NUTS AND PARMESAN

SEARED SALMON OR TUNA CAESAR SALAD

SESAME OIL & RICE VINAIGRETTE SALAD

SLOW ROASTED BEET SALAD

SPINACH SALAD WITH POPPYSEED DRESSING

# CAESAR SALAD

Whenever I make this salad everyone raves, because you can make the dressing a few days ahead and keep it in the refrigerator. The parmesan should be shaved for the best results, but this salad can be made without the parmesan if you want to serve it nondairy. Coarsely grind lots of black pepper on top just before serving. You will need quite a lot of lettuce because it loses volume when you add the dressing.

3 large or 6 small heads of romaine lettuce, broken into large pieces
Croutons
Parmesan (optional)

**DRESSING**
1 egg yolk
2 tsps (10ml) Dijon mustard
1 Tbs (15ml) lemon juice
½ tsp (2.5ml) minced garlic
1 anchovy or 2 Tbs (30ml) capers
Salt
½ cup (125ml) mayonnaise
½ cup (125ml) light olive oil
Freshly ground black pepper

Process all dressing ingredients in food processor, except oil. Drizzle oil down feed tube with motor running. Place lettuce in a mixing bowl and toss with dressing just before serving. Place croutons and parmesan on top just before serving.

NOTE: Dressing can be refrigerated up to 4 days before.

SERVES: 4–6

# CONFETTI SALAD

This is a colorful salad that is very low in fat because the oil content is minimal. It is delightful, delicious and tasty.

2 small baby red cabbages, very finely shredded
2 small baby green cabbages, very finely shredded
4½ oz (150g) fresh spinach, very finely shredded
1 pineapple, julienned
4 medium carrots, julienned
1 medium green papaya, julienned
6 scallions, cut on diagonal
⅓ cup (80ml) toasted sesame seeds
1¾ oz (50g) caramelized pecans or almonds, chopped*

**DRESSING**
4 Tbs (60ml) soft brown sugar
4 Tbs (60ml) light olive oil
1 tsp (5ml) sesame oil
2 Tbs (30ml) freshly chopped ginger
Juice of 1 lemon
6 Tbs (90m) rice vinegar
1 tsp (5ml) salt
Pepper

Mix all salad ingredients together. Just before serving pour over dressing and sesame seeds.

Place on a platter and then sprinkle with chopped nuts.

SERVES: 8–10

NOTE: *If you cannot purchase ready-caramelized nuts, simply make a praline—melt ½ cup sugar with 2 Tbs cold water in a small pot. Bring to a boil and allow to boil until caramel and golden in color. Then pour caramel over pecans or almonds on a baking tray. Allow to cool and harden. When cold chop up into smaller pieces.

Confetti salad

## CREAMY SPINACH SALMON SALAD

I have made this salad for years, and it never ceases to amaze me that the same salad can make people react the way they do whenever they eat it. It makes a wonderful starter salad.

9½ oz (300g) bunch fresh spinach,
  spine removed and very finely shredded
1 red leaf lettuce, shredded very finely
4 hard boiled eggs, coarsely chopped
¼ lb (250g) smoked salmon or trout,
  cut into very fine strips
Croutons

### DRESSING
1 cup (250ml) mayonnaise
½ cup (125ml) cream or nondairy cream
2 Tbs (30ml) white wine vinegar
2 Tbs (30ml) raspberry vinegar or
  sherry vinegar
Salt
Pepper

Whisk all dressing ingredients together. Dressing can be made and kept in fridge for up to 1 week ahead.

Place all salad ingredients except croutons together in a bowl, and place in fridge.

Just before serving toss with dressing and top with croutons.

HANDY TIP: If making individual starter plates leave out salmon and place some on top of salad just before serving.

SERVES: 4–6

## FRESH GRILLED SALMON SALAD

When I made this salad and served it, I was amazed that there was nothing left. It looks outstanding because of the colors of the vegetables. Be careful not to overcook the salmon, as it will dry out as it cools. This salad is best served at room temperature so that the fish does not firm when placed in the refrigerator.

3 sides of fresh salmon with skin on,
  2 lbs (1 kg) each
8½ oz (270g) bottle tartar sauce
½ cup (125ml) creamy herb salad dressing

Preheat oven to grill. Place fish fillets on some pre-sprayed foil on a baking sheet, skin side down. Spread with tartar sauce and salad dressing. Season with salt & pepper.

Grill fish directly under grill for approximately 8 to 10 mins. Do not overcook as fish will dry out. Allow to cool.

2 packets mixed lettuce
½ red pepper, sliced very thinly
½ yellow pepper, sliced very thinly
Some cherry tomatoes
1 avocado, sliced

### DRESSING
¾ cup (175ml) mayonnaise
½ cup (125ml) remainder of herb salad
  dressing
1 tsp (5ml) medium curry powder
1 tsp (5ml) lemon juice
¼ cup (60ml) cold water
Salt and pepper to taste

Place a bed of lettuce on platter. Cut fish in smaller pieces and place in center of platter on top of lettuce. Decorate with peppers, avocado and tomatoes on both sides of the platter. Spoon a little dressing over salad just before serving.

SERVES: 8–10

NOTE: If fish is kept at room temperature and not refrigerated, it is more moist and will not be too cold.

Creamy spinach salmon salad

Fresh grilled salmon salad

# GREEN BEAN, LEEK & POTATO SALAD

*The combination of the vegetables with the mustard dressing makes this an absolute must. It is not a typical potato salad, and looks beautiful spread on a pewter platter. Decorate with a few strips of red pepper or cherry tomatoes for color.*

30 baby potatoes, skin on, cut into wedges
   lengthwise
⅓ cup (80ml) light olive oil
8 oz (250g) very thin green beans,
   blanched for 4 to 5 mins
2 to 3 leeks, (whites only) sliced

Heat oil in a roasting pan in a 400 F (200 C) oven. Season potatoes with salt and pepper and place in roasting pan. Cook for 30 to 40 mins or until slightly browned. Allow to cool.

## DRESSING

⅓ cup (80ml) white vinegar
1 tsp (5ml) minced garlic
2 tsps (10ml) dry rosemary (crushed)
½ cup (125ml) honey mustard salad dressing
1 tsp (5ml) salt
1 egg yolk
¾ cup (175ml) light olive oil

Place all ingredients except oil in food processor. With machine running, add oil in a thin stream allowing dressing to thicken.

Toss over vegetables before serving.

SERVES: 8–10


# GRILLED CORN SALAD

*You will love this salad because of the combination of tastes and textures. The corn, pepper, mushrooms and onions can be grilled a day ahead.*

½ cup (125ml) short brown rice, cooked
6 ears of corn
1 red pepper
2 ripe avocados, quartered
4 oz (125g) mushrooms
8 oz (250g) asparagus
4 oz (125g) green beans
2 onions, cut into thick slices
   (use red onion if available)
Romaine lettuce and cilantro for decoration

Husk corn; boil for 10 minutes. Cut red pepper into strips. Place corn, mushrooms, red pepper and onion in a very hot grilling pan, and grill on all sides until well browned. (May be grilled in oven.) Allow to cool. Set aside.

Blanch asparagus and green beans for a few minutes and place into ice water immediately. Then dry well. Cut corn off the cob, and mix with the red pepper, avocados, mushrooms, asparagus, green beans and onion in a mixing bowl.

Place romaine lettuce on a serving platter. Mound rice on top of lettuce.

Toss remaining ingredients with dressing and place on top of rice and lettuce. Decorate with cilantro.

## DRESSING

1½ cups (325ml) mild salsa
½ cup (125ml) orange juice
⅓ cup (80ml) lemon juice (bottled)
2 Tbs (30ml) ground coriander or
   chopped cilantro
2 tsps (10ml) salt
Pepper
2 Tbs (30ml) olive oil

Whisk dressing ingredients together.

SERVES: 8–10

Green bean, leek & potato salad

Grilled corn salad

## GRILLED VEGETABLE SALAD

*What a colorful addition to an ordinary garden salad these vegetables make. They add color and lots of taste. The vegetables can be broiled the day before, but bring them to room temperature before placing them in the salad.*

1 eggplant, sliced lengthwise
4-5 baby zucchini, sliced lengthwise
3 carrots, sliced lengthwise
8 oz (250g) button mushrooms

1 packet mixed salad greens, broken
1 packet butter lettuce, broken
Shavings of parmesan (if desired)

### DRESSING

⅓ cup (80ml) olive oil
⅓ cup (80ml) sunflower oil
⅓ cup (80ml) balsamic vinegar
1½ tsps (7.5ml) salt
Freshly ground black pepper

TO BROIL VEGETABLES: Salt eggplant, place in colander for ½ hour and then rinse and pat dry. Brush all vegetables with a drop of olive oil. Season with salt and pepper and grill on a baking sheet directly under broiler for a few minutes or until golden. Cool.

Toss salad greens with dressing. Top with grilled vegetables. Drizzle with more dressing.

SERVES: 8–10

## PASTA & ROASTED VEGETABLE SALAD

*The great thing about this salad is that the pasta is small, so there is an abundance of vegetables and this makes it much more than just a pasta salad. You can also serve this as a hot vegetable on its own (for a change of pace).*

8 oz (250g) penne, cooked 'al dente'
4 oz (125g) baby zucchini, sliced thickly
8 oz (250g) button mushrooms, whole
1 red pepper, cut into chunks
1 yellow pepper, cut into chunks
4 oz (125g) baby corn, cut into chunks
2 tomatoes, coarsely chopped
1 onion, coarsely chopped
1 tsp (5ml) minced garlic (optional)
¾ cup (175ml) light olive oil
½ cup (125ml) balsamic vinegar
⅓ cup (80ml) freshly chopped basil
⅔ cup (240g) sun-dried tomatoes in olive oil
½ cup (125ml) sun-dried tomato pesto

Preheat oven to 180 C (375 F).

Cut up vegetables and place in roasting pan. Drizzle with olive oil, balsamic vinegar, minced garlic, basil and salt and pepper.

Roast vegetables uncovered on middle rack of oven for at least 30 to 40 mins or until vegetables are just cooked, seasoning continuously as they absorb a lot of flavor.

Allow to cool. Mix together with cooked penne and sun-dried tomatoes. Adjust seasoning.

SERVES: 8–10

Grilled vegetable salad

## ROASTED MUSHROOM SALAD WITH PINE NUTS AND PARMESAN

*When you want to wow your guests, make this salad because it looks and tastes wonderful. The combination of mushrooms combined with the pine nuts and parmesan shavings, will have your guests raving.*

8 oz (250g) medium brown mushrooms

8 oz (250g) button mushrooms

¾ cup (175ml) light olive oil

⅓ cup (80ml) balsamic vinegar

Salt and pepper

2 tsps (10ml) dry oregano

½ cup (125ml) pine nuts

Parmesan shavings (optional)

Heat oven to 400 F (200 C). Roast mushrooms cap side down on middle rack of oven with oil, balsamic vinegar, salt, pepper and oregano for 30 mins or until mushrooms are soft. Do not overcrowd mushrooms in open roasting pan as they will not brown on the under side.

Place mushrooms in a bowl, and pour over mixture from roasting pan and allow to cool.

Toast pine nuts on a baking sheet in 300 F (140 C) oven for 10 mins or until golden.

Arrange mushrooms on a platter, drizzle with dressing and top with shavings of parmesan and pine nuts just before serving.

SERVES: 6–8

## SEARED SALMON OR TUNA CAESAR SALAD

*This has to be one of my favorite salads. It can be done without the fish and made vegetarian, but the fish adds the finishing touch.*

1 lb (500g) fresh tuna or salmon,
  cut into 3 pieces

2 Tbs (30ml) light soy sauce

1 Tbs (15ml) sesame oil

1 tsp (5ml) sweet chili sauce

1 Tbs (15ml) finely minced ginger

2 small heads romaine lettuce,
  broken into pieces

1 red pepper, chopped

4 oz (125g) baby corn, blanched and cut
  [or 1 14-oz can (410g tin) baby corn]

1 cup (250ml) pine nuts or slivered almonds

Sliced avocado

Croutons

¾ cup (175ml) grated parmesan or feta

Salt and pepper

### DRESSING

⅓ cup (80ml) fresh lemon juice

1 Tbs (15ml) soft brown sugar

1 Tbs (15ml) light soya sauce

1 Tbs (15ml) mayonnaise

½ cup (125ml) olive oil

1 tsp (5ml) sweet chili sauce*

½ tsp (2.5ml) salt

½ tsp (2.5ml) minced garlic (optional)

Combine soy, sesame oil, chili sauce and ginger. Add fish and allow to marinate at least 15 mins.

Toast pine nuts in oven at 300 F (140 C) for 8 to 10 mins. Blend all dressing ingredients together until smooth. Refrigerate.

Place lettuce, red pepper, corn, nuts and avocado on a platter.

Heat a wok or frying pan. When very hot, add 2 Tbs olive oil and allow to smoke. Add fish and sear on both sides until almost cooked through. Slice fish.

Scatter fish on top of salad greens. Drizzle salad dressing over. Sprinkle with parmesan or feta, salt and pepper.

SERVES: 8–10

* See substitutes

Roasted mushroom salad with pine nuts and parmesan

## SESAME OIL & RICE VINAIGRETTE SALAD

*As simple as this salad seems, it is the dressing that makes it. Your guests will rave about the dressing, so show off and impress them. The dressing can be made a few days ahead and kept in the refrigerator.*

1 head butter lettuce, broken into pieces
1 head iceberg lettuce, broken into pieces
9 oz (300g) baby cucumbers,
   cut into thin strips
7 oz (200g) peeled baby carrots, cut smaller
7 oz (200g) red cherry tomatoes
1 avocado
Croutons

### DRESSING
⅓ cup (80ml) sunflower oil
4 Tbs (60ml) light sesame oil
⅓ cup (80ml) rice vinegar*
2 tsps (10ml) dark soy sauce
1 tsp (5ml) salt
2 tsps (10ml) sugar
1 tsp (5ml) garlic salt
4 Tbs (30ml) mayonnaise
¼ cup (60ml) cold water
1 tsp (5ml) French dijon mustard

Whisk all dressing ingredients together and pour over salad just before serving.

Dressing will keep in fridge for up to 10 days. Pour just enough dressing over to coat salad.

* See substitute

SERVES: 8–10

## SLOW ROASTED BEET SALAD

*Since beets don't suit all tastes, do not make too much. Rather serve a mound of beets in the center with the salad surrounding it. This salad is a stunner. The flavor of the orange rind, the balsamic and the brown sugar all come through from the roasting process. You'll love it.*

8 to 10 whole beets, cut into quarters
   (or baby beets)

¼ cup (60ml) olive oil
¼ cup (60ml) balsamic vinegar
Juice of 1 orange
2 Tbs (30ml) orange rind
¼ cup (60ml) soft brown sugar

Preheat oven to 350 F (160 C).

Place beets uncovered in small roasting pan. Sprinkle with all above ingredients. Season very well with salt and pepper.

Roast for 1 hour. Turn oven down to 325 F (140 C) and continue roasting for a further 30 to 40 minutes or until beets are soft.

Whisk additional ⅓ cup (80ml) olive oil and ¼ cup (60ml) balsamic and ¼ cup (60ml) orange juice. Adjust seasoning and add more salt and pepper, if desired. Drizzle half dressing over beets. Reserve remaining dressing for lettuce.

Serve in the center of a lettuce, tomato, carrot and deep fried leek salad.

SERVES: 8

TO SERVE: Deep fry some very thinly sliced leeks. Toss mixed lettuce with dressing and surround beets with lettuce. Top with fried leeks.

## SPINACH SALAD WITH POPPYSEED DRESSING

This dressing has a wonderful orange flavor that permeates the salad. I love making it because it is colorful as well as being very tasty.

1 lb (500g) button mushrooms

3 Tbs (45ml) light olive oil

Salt and freshly ground black pepper

9½ oz (300g) baby spinach
  (or Japanese sweet spinach if available),
  broken into pieces

1 large head romaine or butter lettuce,
  broken into pieces

2 hard boiled eggs, chopped

1 red onion, sliced thinly

⅓ cup (80ml) pine nuts, toasted

1 avocado, sliced

Sauté mushrooms in olive oil until dry, seasoning while cooking. Set aside to cool. Mix all salad ingredients, except avocado, lightly together in a mixing bowl.

### DRESSING

1 tsp (5ml) salt

½ cup (125ml) olive oil

⅓ cup (80ml) white wine vinegar

½ tsp (2.5ml) sugar or sweetener

Ground black pepper

1 Tbs (15ml) poppy seeds

4 Tbs (60ml) mayonnaise

½ cup (125ml) fresh orange juice

Whisk all dressing ingredients together. Dress salad just before serving.

Dressing can be made up to 4 days before and refrigerated.

SERVES: 8–10

Slow roasted beet salad

Salmon cakes with avocado butter

HOT NORI FISH ROLLS

SALMON CAKES WITH AVOCADO BUTTER

# FISH

SOLE WITH MUSHROOM SAUCE

WHOLE BAKED FISH WITH HERBS

Fish is a very light, low-fat, yet filling dish that lends itself to a variety of spices and sauces. Many different cooking methods are possible when using it.

Always remember that the fresher the fish is, the tastier it will be. I do not like frozen fish as it retains a lot of water.

For best results, fish should be cooked and served immediately. It does not lend itself to cooking ahead of time as it becomes dry.

To cook fish to perfection, it should be cooked for 10 minutes per ½ inch (1cm) of thickness at the thickest part of the fish. When pierced with a fork, the fork should not meet with resistance. Salmon, however, should always be slightly undercooked and a little bit pink; otherwise it becomes very dry.

Ginger glazed salmon

# FISH

CRUMBED PINK SALMON WITH SPICY MAYONNAISE

WRAPPED FISH BAKE

GINGER-LIME GLAZED SALMON WITH JULIENNED VEGETABLES

GRILLED SALMON WITH RED PEPPER MAYONNAISE

HOT NORI FISH ROLLS

SALMON IN SAFFRON SAUCE WITH COUSCOUS

ROASTED SEA BASS WITH GRILLED MUSHROOMS AND POTATOES

SALMON CAKES WITH AVOCADO BUTTER

SOLE WITH MUSHROOM SAUCE

WHOLE BAKED FISH PACKET WITH HERBS

WHOLE BAKED SEA BASS WITH MUSTARD MAYONNAISE

## CRUMBED PINK SALMON WITH SPICY MAYONNAISE

*One of my all time favorites that I keep forgetting about. A simple, uncomplicated main course that is really sensational. Be careful not to overcook the salmon. If you are using tuna, or another fish that is thicker than salmon, the cooking time will be longer.*

2 lbs (1 kg) salmon fillets, skin on

¼ cup (60ml) chopped parsley

⅓ cup (80ml) grated parmesan or crumbled
  pecorino

¼ cup (60ml) freshly chopped thyme
  or 1 Tbs (15ml) dried thyme

1 tsp (5ml) grated lemon rind

½ tsp (2.5ml) salt

1 tsp (5ml) minced garlic

1½ cups (375ml) breadcrumbs

6 Tbs (90ml) melted butter or margarine

Preheat oven to 375 F (180 C).

Process parsley, thyme, parmesan, lemon rind and salt in food processor. Add garlic and then breadcrumbs. Stir in melted butter.

Pat salmon dry. Place a piece of foil on a baking sheet, dull side up. Spray with nonstick cooking spray. Place fish on foil, skin side down. Pat crumb mixture on top of fillets.

Bake for 10 mins. Then turn grill on, place fish slightly closer to grill and watch carefully for a few seconds until golden.

Serve with spicy mayonnaise.

### SPICY MAYONNAISE

⅓ cup (80ml) parsley

¼ cup (60ml) chopped spring onion

2 Tbs (30ml) red wine vinegar

½ tsp (2.5ml) oregano

Freshly ground black pepper

Dash of cayenne pepper

1 cup (250ml) mayonnaise

Combine all ingredients and allow to sit for at least 30 mins. Serve with fish.

SERVES: 4

## WRAPPED FISH BAKE

*When you think of a pie you think of a round dish covered with pastry. This is more like a strudel and tastes and looks absolutely delicious because of all the colored vegetables.*

2 large leeks, sliced thinly (white only)

2 Tbs (30ml) olive oil

4 oz (125g) brown mushrooms, sliced and sautéed

2 lb (1kg) salmon fillets, cut into thick chunks

3 Tbs (45ml) dill, freshly chopped

3 Tbs (45ml) parsley, freshly chopped

3 Tbs (45ml) olive oil

½ cup (125ml) julienned carrots

4 oz (125g) fresh asparagus,
  cut into smaller pieces (about 10)

21 oz (600g) roll frozen puff pastry (1½ rolls)

1 egg beaten with 1 Tbs water

Sauté leeks in olive oil until brown. Then add mushrooms and sauté until quite dry. Set aside.

Cut fish into large pieces and toss with dill, parsley and lots of seasoning. Sauté fish with carrots on high heat for a few minutes. Then add cooled leeks, mushrooms and asparagus. Season well. Drain excess juice.

Preheat oven to 400 F (200 C). Line a baking sheet with baking paper. Spray the paper.

Roll out 1 packet puff pastry. Place on baking paper. Spread filling on top of pastry leaving a 1½ to 2-inch (4-5 cm) border around the edges. Roll out remaining ½ packet pastry. Place on top of the filling.

Brush the border of the pastry with the beaten egg mixture. Fold in borders, pinching to fit on to top piece of pastry. Brush entire outside of pastry with egg.

Bake uncovered for 20 minutes or until golden.

SERVES: 6–8

Crumbed pink salmon with spicy mayonnaise

# GINGER-LIME GLAZED SALMON WITH JULIENNED VEGETABLES

The combination of lime juice, soy sauce and seasonings give the fish a wonderful color as well as taste. This combined with the vegetables makes this fish dish a special meal.

3 lbs (1.5kg) salmon, filleted with skin on

2 Tbs (30ml) fresh chopped ginger
¼ cup (60ml) fresh lime juice
  (or bottled lemon if unavailable)
2 Tbs (30ml) dark soy sauce
1 tsp (5ml) seasoning salt
Black pepper
4 oz (125g) salted butter, softened

Preheat grill in oven.

Make a paste with above ingredients. Place fish skin side down on a sprayed piece of foil on a baking sheet. Spread mixture on to fish and place it in middle of oven under grill for 8-10 mins or until fish is slightly undercooked. This must be done just before serving.

## VEGETABLES
## (ALL CUT INTO VERY THIN LONG STRIPS)

½ red pepper
4 oz (125g) thin green beans
½ yellow pepper
4 oz (125g) snow peas (mangetouts)
1 leek or scallion
2 carrots, julienned
4 oz (125g) baby corn
2 sticks celery
8 oz (250g) very thin asparagus

## SAUCE

2 Tbs (30ml) sweet chili sauce*
¼ cup (60ml) soy sauce
2 Tbs (30ml) tomato sauce
¼ cup (60ml) rice vinegar
3 Tbs (45ml) soft brown sugar
1 Tbs (15ml) cornstarch (maizena),
  dissolved in 3 Tbs cold water

Stir-fry carrots and celery first in a little oil in a heated wok. Add remaining vegetables except peppers and baby corn. Stir-fry very quickly just to wilt. Remove from wok and place in a colander to drain excess liquid.

In the same wok, bring all sauce ingredients to a boil and thicken slightly with cornstarch. Add peppers and corn. Toss with vegetables and sauce.

TO SERVE: Slide fish off baking sheet on to platter and surround with vegetables.

NOTE: Alternatively, do not cook vegetables at all. Place them with the sauce in the microwave and heat for 5 to 8 minutes on high just before serving.

SERVES: 4–6
* See substitutes

Ginger-lime glazed salmon with julienned vegetables

## GRILLED SALMON WITH RED PEPPER MAYONNAISE

There is nothing nicer than a fresh grilled piece of fish and this sauce gives it the finishing touch.

3 lbs (1.5kg) fresh salmon fillet or sea bass
  (skin on), or tuna (without skin)
Herbamare, olive oil, paprika
Freshly ground black papper

Preheat grill in oven.

Brush skin side of fish with a little olive oil. Place fish on sprayed foil on a baking sheet with the skin side down. Then brush flesh side of fish with olive oil just to coat lightly.

Season well with Herbamare, paprika and pepper. Grill fish as below!

NOTE:
SALMON: Needs to grill higher up and closer to the element as it is thinner. Do not turn fish. Grill only for 5 to 8 mins. Then remove from oven.

FRESH TUNA: Needs to grill in center of oven or it will burn. Turn halfway during cooking. Season other side. Allow 10 to 12 mins each side. Fish is cooked when pierced with a fork; the fork must go through easily.

SEA BASS: Needs to grill in middle to upper part of oven. Do not turn. Season one side only. Grill for approx. 15 mins.

NOTE: ALWAYS UNDERCOOK FISH SLIGHTLY IN ORDER NOT TO DRY IT OUT. SERVE WITH RED PEPPER SAUCE SEPARATELY.

### RED PEPPER SAUCE

½ cup (60ml) mayonnaise
½ fresh red pepper, cut into strips
2 Tbs (15ml) red onion or scallion
¼ cup (60ml) fresh parsley
2 Tbs (30ml) fresh cilantro
2 tsps (10ml) capers, drained
1 Tbs (15ml) coarse grain honey mustard
1 Tbs (15ml) sun-dried tomatoes, chopped
1 Tbs (15ml) lemon juice
1 tsp (5ml) salt
Freshly ground black pepper

Place all ingredients in a food processor and process until quite smooth. Refrigerate. Can be made 2 days ahead.

SERVES: 4–6

## HOT NORI FISH ROLLS

An easy alternative to raw sushi—for the not so daring.

3 sheets of nori (seaweed)
9½ oz (300g) fresh halibut, cut into 6 long strips
9½ oz (300g) fresh salmon,
  cut into 6 long strips
9 raw fresh asparagus, lightly blanched
Scallion, cut into long strips
Herbamare, pepper, salt

Place a sheet of nori on a bamboo rolling mat. In center of nori, place 2 thin strips of fresh halibut lengthwise. Place 2 asparagus in between. Season. Top with salmon and scallion pieces. Turn rolling mat.

Roll up tightly and rub a little rice vinegar on the end of the nori roll to seal. Place whole roll in fridge for a few minutes. Continue making more rolls until fish is finished. Place refrigerated rolls on a sprayed cooling rack, on top of a baking sheet. Bake in preheated 375 F (180 C) oven for 10 minutes.

Allow to cool and then cut into thick slices. Serve with pickled ginger mayonnaise and wasabi. (If desired.)

TO SERVE WITH ROLLS:
1 Tbs (15ml) pickled ginger
½ cup (125ml) mayonnaise

Place ginger and mayonnaise in food processor until blended.

SERVES: 6

Hot nori fish rolls

## SALMON IN SAFFRON SAUCE WITH COUSCOUS

*You'll amaze them with this wonderful sauce, fish and vegetable combination.*

4½ lbs (2kg) salmon, filleted and skinned
4 Tbs (60g) butter
Salt, pepper, paprika

Melt butter in a large frying pan. Cut fish into large serving size portions of approx. 8 oz (200-250g) each. Season with salt, pepper and paprika. Lightly sauté fish on medium-high for 5 to 8 minutes each side depending on the thickness of the fish.

Fish can be slightly undercooked and then finished on a baking sheet, in a hot 400 F (200 C) oven. Must be served immediately.

### SAFFRON SAUCE

4 Tbs (60g) unsalted butter
2 leeks, finely chopped
1 tsp (5ml) minced garlic
1 cup (250ml) dry white wine
½ cup (125ml) white cinzano (or sweet wine)
1 packet saffron [or ½ tsp (2.5ml) turmeric or
  generous pinch saffron threads]
1 cup (250ml) vegetable stock
  (½ Knorr or 1 Telma cube)
1½ cups (375ml) cream
Salt and black pepper

Sauté leeks and garlic in butter until soft. Add wine, cinzano and saffron and reduce in a large open frying pan or pot on high heat for approx. 8 mins.

Add stock and reduce again by half. Lastly add cream and reduce on medium-low heat until quite thick and mixture coats a spoon. (If you reduce cream on high heat it will boil over. Strain sauce before serving.)

NOTE: Sauce can be made a few days ahead and reheated gently on low heat.

### COUSCOUS

4 Tbs (60g) butter
½ green or yellow pepper,
  very finely chopped
½ red pepper, very finely chopped
1 cup (250ml) couscous
1 cup (250ml) vegetable or chicken stock
  (½ Knorr or 1 Telma cube)
2 Tbs (30ml) olive oil

Sauté peppers in butter until softened. Set aside. Bring stock and oil to a boil. Pour in couscous and remove from stove, but cover with lid of pot. Allow to swell for 2 mins. Stir in peppers and set aside.

TO SERVE: Place couscous on a platter. Top with fish and spoon over sauce. Decorate with freshly chopped parsley.

SERVES: 10

## ROASTED SEA BASS WITH GRILLED MUSHROOMS AND POTATOES

*What a great taste the mushroom and potatoes give the fish!*

2 lbs (1kg) sea bass fillet, cut in half,
  to make two thinner pieces
¼ cup (60ml) flour
1 Tbs (15ml) cornstarch (maizena)
½ tsp (2.5ml) peri-peri powder
  [or ¼ tsp (1.5ml) chili powder]
1 tsp (5ml) garlic salt
Herbamare (if available)
Coarse salt
Seasoning salt

Mix together the flour, cornstarch and spices. Dip fish into this mixture. Heat 1 Tbs (15ml) butter and 2 Tbs (30ml) olive oil in a frying pan until very hot.

Quickly brown fish on each side for 2 minutes, then place on a sprayed baking sheet and set aside.

## VEGETABLES

8 baby potatoes, cut in half lengthwise

8 oz (250g) button mushrooms, whole

8 oz (250g) medium brown mushrooms, whole

Olive oil

Coarse salt and pepper

Place potatoes in a roasting pan. Season generously with olive oil, coarse salt and pepper and roast on 425 F (220 C) for approx. ½ hour. Remove and set aside on a plate. Place mushrooms in same pan and roast with olive oil, salt, pepper and seasoning until quite dry—approx. 20 mins. Set aside with potatoes.

## SAUCE

1 cup (250ml) semi-sweet wine

2 cups (500ml) vegetable stock
  (1 Knorr or 2 Telma cubes)

2 tsps (10ml) mustard powder

1 egg yolk

½ cup (125ml) cream

3 scallions, finely chopped

2 tsps (10ml) freshly chopped parsley

2 Tbs (30ml) lemon juice

1 Tbs (15ml) coarse grain mustard (optional)

Place wine in a medium pot and boil on high to reduce by half for about 5 mins. Then add vegetable stock and reduce for a further 10 mins to make 1½ cups. Whisk in mustard powder.

Remove some liquid and whisk in egg yolk to avoid curdling. Whisk cream into egg yolk mixture. Place egg yolk mixture back in pot and allow to thicken on medium high heat. Stir in scallions, parsley, lemon juice and coarse mustard to complete the sauce. Season to taste.

JUST BEFORE SERVING: Place fish in middle of oven under grill to complete cooking. Heat vegetables in oven. Reheat sauce. Place vegetables on platter. Top with fish. Spoon over sauce.

# SALMON CAKES WITH AVOCADO BUTTER

A platterful of these fish cakes make an elegant buffet dish. Your guests will love them. They also make a delicious everyday light meal.

1 lb (500g) deboned cooked cod, flaked

6 oz (213g) can pink salmon, cleaned

2 eggs, beaten

2 Tbs (30ml) chopped parsley

2 Tbs (30ml) coarse grain mustard

Drop of Worcestershire Sauce

2 Tbs (30ml) chopped scallion

½ cup (125ml) matzo meal [or ⅓ cup (80ml) breadcrumbs]

¼ cup (60ml) mayonnaise

Juice of ½ lemon

½ tsp (2.5ml) chili powder

Salt and pepper

1 onion sliced and sautéed in oil until brown

¼ - ½ cup (60-125ml) water (if necessary to make mixture more spongy)

Sauté onion in a little oil until browned. Remove and set aside. (This adds flavor to the oil.) Combine salmon, cod and all other ingredients. Season to taste. Shape into patties and fry in shallow, hot oil for a few minutes or until browned on each side. Do not turn too many times, as patties will break. Drain on paper towel.

MAKES 24 PATTIES

## AVOCADO BUTTER

1 large avocado

2 Tbs (30ml) lemon juice

2 Tbs (30ml) tartar sauce

½ tomato

Salt and pepper

Process all ingredients in food processor until smooth. Place a drop of avocado butter on each salmon cake and serve with lemon wedges on a bed of butter lettuce and sautéed onion.

## SOLE WITH MUSHROOM SAUCE

*This makes a most elegant yet simple dinner dish. It is very yummy.*

8 small sole fillets
1 small onion, finely chopped
1 tsp (5ml) minced garlic
2 Tbs (30ml) butter
1 Tbs (15ml) flour
½ cup (125ml) vegetable stock
  (½ Knorr or 1 Telma cube)
½ cup (125ml) dry white wine
2 Tbs (30ml) lemon juice
1 lb (250g) white mushrooms, sliced
1 egg yolk
1 Tbs (15ml) cream
1 Tbs (15ml) parsley, chopped

Sauté onion and garlic in butter until soft. Whisk in flour. Then add stock, wine and lemon juice and allow to boil, stirring continuously for 5 mins until thick. Add mushrooms and cook until softened.

Beat a little mushroom sauce with egg yolk and cream. Then add this entire mixture to remaining mushroom sauce in pan. Reheat gently without boiling. Add chopped parsley.

Dip sole into seasoned flour (salt and pepper). Fry in a little browned butter or olive oil, turning once. Arrange sole on platter and drizzle sauce across them.

SERVES: 4–6

## WHOLE BAKED FISH PACKET WITH HERBS

*A delicious herb-infused fish dish!*

2½ lb (1.5kg) whole trout or sea bass,
  butterflied, with head and tail
3 Tbs (50g) butter or margarine
2 Tbs (30ml) olive oil
4 Tbs (60ml) dill, freshly chopped
2 Tbs (30ml) basil, freshly chopped
Generous seasoning for flavor,
  paprika, coarse salt, pepper, etc.
Fresh lemon juice (2 lemons)

Make a paste with the butter, olive oil and herbs. Season the paste very well. Place the fish in a double layer of heavy foil on the dull side, which has been sprayed with nonstick cooking spray (or with olive oil spray).

Spread paste over entire fish as well as the middle of the fish. Pour over some fresh lemon juice. Seal foil tightly. Place on a baking tray in a preheated 400 F (200 C) oven on the middle rack for 20 to 25 mins.

HANDY TIP: When your fork pierces fish easily with no resistance, then fish is cooked through. Serve immediately.

SERVES: 6

## WHOLE BAKED SEA BASS WITH MUSTARD MAYONNAISE

*I have made this fish many times over the years, and it is always one of the tastiest and top favorites. The flesh of the fish remains so tender, and the mayonnaise keeps the moisture inside the fish. It looks stunning on a buffet table.*

4.5 lbs (2kg) whole sea bass or other line
  fish, butterflied, center bone removed, but
  with head and tail
2 cups (500ml) mayonnaise
4 Tbs (60ml) coarse grain mustard
4 Tbs (60ml) Dijon mustard
Salt and pepper

Preheat oven to 400 F (200 C).

Mix all ingredients together.

Place fish on a baking sheet covered in heavy foil and sprayed with nonstick cooking spray. Spread a little mayonnaise mixture on inside of fish. Season well. Close fish and spread more mayonnaise on outside of one side of fish (skin side up) excluding head and tail. Season very well. Cook on middle rack for 15 mins. Then switch on grill, move fish up slightly and grill until brown.

TO TURN FISH: Place a second baking sheet covered with foil and sprayed on top of the fish and invert it on to the new baking sheet.

Spread other side of fish with mayonnaise mixture, season very well and grill until well browned. Reduce oven temp to 400 F (200 C) and cook fish a further 10 mins or until a fork goes through fish easily.

SERVES: 8–10

Whole baked fish packet with herbs

Salmon in saffron sauce with couscous

Roasted sea bass with grilled mushrooms and potatoes

Whole baked sea bass with mustard mayonnaise

Roasted pumpkin and mascarpone crooked pasta

FRESH PORCINI PASTA

TOMATO & MOZZARELLA SHELL PASTA

# PASTAS

SPINACH AND RICOTTA GNOCCHI

PENNE ARRABBIATA

Whether baked or unbaked, pasta dishes are wholesome and nutritious. They simply require a beautiful tossed salad and some fresh, crispy bread to complete the meal.

Always boil pasta in a large pot of water with lots of salt and a drop of oil. This stops the pasta from sticking together. Particularly in pasta dishes that are not sauced, the salt in the water adds flavor to the pasta.

Fresh pasta is lighter than dried pasta, and cooks much quicker. When you are going to bake a pasta dish, then your pasta must be slightly undercooked "al dente," because it will cook again.

# PASTAS

ANGEL-HAIR PASTA WITH SPINACH AND SLIVERED ALMONDS

FARFALLE WITH CHEESE AND MUSHROOMS

FETTUCINE WITH BAKED RICOTTA & CARAMELIZED ONIONS

FRESH PORCINI PASTA

GRILLED VEGETABLE PASTA BAKE

MUSHROOM AND RICOTTA CANNELONI

MUSHROOM, ASPARAGUS & CORN FETTUCINE

PENNE ARRABBIATA

ROASTED PUMPKIN & MASCARPONE CROOKED PASTA

SPINACH AND RICOTTA GNOCCHI

TOMATO & MOZZARELLA SHELL PASTA

## ANGEL-HAIR PASTA WITH SPINACH AND SLIVERED ALMONDS

*The texture of crunchy almonds with pasta and spinach makes a delicious combination. If you don't want a saucy pasta, this is lovely and light because it is just tossed with olive oil.*

7 oz (200g) slivered or flaked almonds

½ cup (125ml) olive oil

2 tsps (10ml) minced garlic

Pinch of cayenne pepper

7½ oz (300g) bunch of fresh spinach,
  stems removed and coarsely chopped

4 Tbs (60g) butter or margarine

1 cup (250ml) grated parmesan cheese

Salt and pepper

13 oz (375g) angel-hair pasta
  (tagliatellini, very thin spaghetti)

Place almonds on a baking sheet and toast in a preheated 300 F (140 C) oven for 8 to 10 minutes.

Heat the oil in a pan and sauté garlic and cayenne pepper. Remove from heat. Add chopped spinach and toss over high heat for 1 min to wilt. Stir in butter or margarine.

Just before serving, bring water to boil in a large pot with salt and a drop of oil. Cook pasta until 'al dente.' Drain very well. Place in a large bowl.

Add spinach, parmesan and nuts and season to taste with salt and pepper.

Serve immediately.

SERVES: 6–8

## FARFALLE WITH CHEESE AND MUSHROOMS

*This wonderful baked pasta dish can be made up to 2 days ahead and then baked when you need it. Farfalle makes a stunning dish.*

8 oz (250g) cooked farfalle pasta, 'al dente'

½ cup (125ml) chopped onion

½ tsp (2.5ml) minced garlic

½ tsp (2.5ml) dry chili flakes

8 oz (250g) button mushrooms, sliced

8 oz (250g) medium brown mushrooms, sliced

1 tsp (5ml) dry basil

1 tsp (5ml) dry oregano

2 Tbs (30ml) olive oil

4 Tbs (60g) unsalted butter or margarine

2 Tbs (30ml) flour

1 cup (250ml) lowfat milk

14-oz can (1 x 410g tin) whole peeled
  tomatoes, chopped with liquid

½ cup (125ml) feta cheese, crumbled

½ cup (125ml) cheddar cheese, grated

½ cup (125ml) emmentaler or Swiss cheese, grated

⅓ cup (80ml) grated parmesan or pecorino

¼ cup (60ml) freshly chopped parsley

In a large frying pan, sauté the onion, garlic, chili flakes, basil, oregano in the oil until onion is softened. Add sliced mushrooms, cook until softened and some liquid has evaporated. Set aside in a mixing bowl.

In the same pan, melt butter. Whisk in the flour and stir for 1 min. Add milk, whisking until thickened. Season with salt and pepper.

Pour white sauce over mushrooms. Add chopped tomatoes. Mix together and add cheese. Taste for seasoning.

Rinse farfalle with cold water to separate them, or they will break. Drain and toss with rest of mixture.

Place in a pre-sprayed ovenproof dish. Top with grated parmesan. Oven must be preheated to 400 F (200 C). Bake on middle shelf for 25 to 30 mins or until bubbling.

HANDY TIP: Can be frozen before baking. Defrost before baking as above. Can be made and kept in refrigerator for 2 to 3 days ahead.

SERVES: 8–10

## FETTUCINE WITH BAKED RICOTTA & CARAMELIZED ONIONS

*I love the combination of sweet onions, salty ricotta and red pepper with this pasta. The ricotta cake can be made ahead and reheated, the onions caramelized and the red pepper sautéed the day before, so you will be able to make pasta in record time, and it will taste delicious.*

8 oz (250g) fettucine
2 to 3 Tbs (30 to 45ml) olive oil
Black pepper

1¼ lbs (350g) ricotta cheese
3.5 oz (100g) black pepper feta
2 eggs
2 Tbs (30ml) flour
Salt, pepper, ground herbs

Preheat oven to 400 F (200 C).

Mix ricotta, feta, eggs, flour, seasoning and herbs together. Place mixture in a sprayed pie dish and bake 25 mins or until firm to touch. Cool slightly. Slice ricotta into wedges. Place on a platter. Keep warm.

1 red pepper, sliced thinly and sautéed in a frying pan with a little olive oil and seasoned until softened
6 red onions, sliced
(use white if red unavailable)
3 Tbs (45ml) olive oil
2 Tbs (30ml) brown sugar
3½ oz (100g) black pepper or plain feta

Cook sliced red onions in olive oil over medium heat for at least 20 to 30 mins or until golden and softened. Stir in brown sugar at end to caramelize.

Cook pasta. Drain.

Toss cooked pasta with olive oil and season with salt and pepper. Toss with caramelized onions, peppers and with an additional 3½ oz (100g) black pepper feta.

Sprinkle with some chives or scallions, finely sliced and some chopped parsley. Place mixed pasta on top of ricotta wedges and serve immediately.

SERVES: 6–8

## FRESH PORCINI PASTA

*The beauty of this dish is its simplicity. You must use fresh porcini mushrooms because of their marvelous taste. If asparagus is not in season, then simply leave it out. This pasta is sensational, and also makes a wonderful starter.*

8 oz (250g) trenette (or thin fettucine)

4 to 5 large fresh porcini mushrooms
2 cloves garlic, slivered
1 cup (250ml) light olive oil
8 oz (250g) fresh asparagus,
  cut into ¼-inch (2-cm) pieces
Coarse salt and pepper
Freshly grated parmesan or feta (optional)

Heat olive oil. Add garlic slivers and sauté until crisp. Place thickly sliced mushrooms in oil and sauté until softened. Season generously with coarse salt and pepper.

Add asparagus. Continue cooking until just done. Set aside.

Boil pasta in quite salty water to give the pasta taste. Toss pasta with olive oil and mushroom/asparagus mixture. Sprinkle with grated parmesan and lots of black pepper. Serve immediately.

SERVES: 6–8

## GRILLED VEGETABLE PASTA BAKE

*My children love vegetables and pasta, so I created a combination of the two without a very fattening sauce to make this delectable, wholesome dish.*

1 lb (500g) rigatoni

Cook rigatoni, but undercook slightly. Rinse with cold water. Toss with 1 Tbs (15ml) olive oil. Set aside.

8 oz (250g) white mushrooms, sliced thinly
6 small baby zucchini, sliced thinly

2 small red onions, sliced
  (or 4 scallions, sliced)
8 oz (250g) baby butternut (if available),
  sliced in rounds
4 oz (125g) baby corn, cut in half
4 oz (125g) snow peas, cut in half
1 red pepper, sliced thinly
14-oz can (1 X 410g tin) diced tomatoes, drained
2 Tbs (30ml) olive oil
1½ tsps (7.5ml) Herbamare or other seasoning
2 Tbs (30ml) freshly chopped basil

Place all vegetables in a roasting pan except snow peas. Preheat oven to grill and place rack in center to upper part of oven. Add canned tomatoes, olive oil, Herbamare and basil. Position under grill and allow to brown. Continue turning vegetables until nearly done and browned approx. 20 mins. Remove from oven and add snow peas.

### WHITE SAUCE
2 cups (500ml) vegetable stock
  (2 Knorr or 3 Telma cubes)
3 Tbs (45ml) flour, dissolved in a little water
1-2 cups (250-500ml) lowfat milk
3 cups (750ml) cheddar cheese
Pepper

Bring vegetable stock to a boil in a medium pot. Whisk in flour and allow to thicken. Then add milk, cheese and seasoning and set aside.

Mix ¾ sauce with the precooked pasta. Mix remaining white sauce with vegetables.

Preheat oven to 375 F (180 C).

Spray an open ovenproof dish. Place half the vegetables in a dish, top with pasta, then add more vegetables and finish with pasta. Sprinkle with a little additional grated cheese and some parmesan cheese.

Bake on middle rack of oven for 25 to 30 mins or until bubbling. Serve immediately.

NOTE: Can be prepared 2 days ahead and kept in refrigerator. Bring to room temperature before baking.

SERVES: 10–12

Angel-hair pasta with spinach and slivered almonds

Farfalle with cheese and mushrooms

Fettucine with baked ricotta & caramelized onions

Grilled vegetable pasta bake

# MUSHROOM AND RICOTTA CANNELONI

The trick to using canneloni shells that don't require any cooking, is to have enough liquid in the dish. The canneloni must be well covered with the sauce, or it will be hard on top. You can substitute spinach for the mushrooms if you desire. You will love the flavors of this delicious dish.

1 onion, finely chopped

2 Tbs (30ml) olive oil

8 oz (250g) button mushrooms, chopped

8 oz (250g) brown mushrooms

8 oz (250g) ricotta cheese
  (or chunky cottage cheese)

1 egg, beaten

1 cup (250ml) cheddar cheese, grated

¾ cup (175ml) grated parmesan or feta

Salt and pepper

Sauté onions in olive oil until softened. Add mushrooms and sauté until quite dry. Season well with salt and pepper. Remove from stove and stir in ricotta or cottage cheese, cheddar cheese, parmesan, beaten egg and seasoning.

Place mushrooms and cheese mixture in a piping bag with a large nozzle and pipe filling into canneloni tubes.

## WHITE SAUCE

3 Tbs (45ml) butter

3 Tbs (45ml) flour

1½ cups (375ml) milk

Salt, pepper and nutmeg

Melt butter in a pot. Add flour and stir for 1 min to cook. Slowly add milk and whisk to remove any lumps. Season with salt, pepper and ½ tsp (2.5ml) nutmeg. Mix with tomato sauce.

2 to 3 cups (500 to 750ml) ready-cooked tomato sauce

4 oz (½ box or 125g) canneloni, uncooked and ready to use

Preheat oven to 375 F (180 C).

Place half of sauce on bottom of a pre-sprayed ovenproof dish. Line filled tubes next to each other on top of sauce. Cover generously with more sauce. Sprinkle with grated parmesan.

Bake uncovered on middle rack of oven for 25 to 30 mins or until soft when pricked with a fork.

HANDY TIP: To ensure canneloni is soft, cover with a lot of sauce. Can be made ahead of time but do not bake. If frozen, defrost first and then bake until brown and bubbling. Be careful that the sauce does not dry up.

SERVES: 10–12

Mushroom and ricotta canneloni

## MUSHROOM, ASPARAGUS & CORN FETTUCINE

There is nothing nicer than fresh vegetables tossed with a light creamy fettucine. The richness of the sherry, wine and cream permeates this delicious pasta.

8 oz (250g) fettucine

4 Tbs (60ml) olive oil
16 oz (500g) brown mushrooms, sliced
½ cup (125ml) sherry (medium cream)
½ cup (25ml) white wine (not too dry)
2 cups (500ml) vegetable stock
  (1 Knorr or 2 Telma cubes)
1 cup (250ml) cream
Freshly ground black pepper
2 Tbs (30ml) fresh chives
2 Tbs (30ml) freshly chopped parsley
8 oz (250g) fresh asparagus, cut into pieces
7 oz (200g) baby corn, blanched or
  14 oz (410g) canned baby corn
½ cup (125ml) grated parmesan
1 tsp (5ml) Herbamare or other seasoning

Sauté mushrooms in olive oil in a large frying pan until dry. Season well with salt and pepper. Add white wine and sherry. Reduce by half by boiling on medium-high heat without the lid. Then add stock and reduce again for a further 5 minutes. Add cream and allow to boil again until thickened slightly. Add chives, parsley and Herbamare.

Stir in asparagus and corn only when sauce is hot.

Boil pasta and drain. Toss with a drop of olive oil and then toss with sauce and vegetables.

HANDY TIP: Sauce can be made ahead of time and reheated on a low temperature. Only add asparagus and corn when reheating.

SERVES: 6–8

## PENNE ARRABBIATA

This simple pasta dish is always successful no matter when you make it. The sauce freezes very well, so make it in quantity and keep it in the freezer. The longer and slower you cook the sauce, the more flavor it has.

8 oz (250g) penne, cooked 'al dente'

1 onion, chopped finely
1 tsp (5ml) minced garlic
1 tsp (5ml) chili paste
¼ cup (60ml) olive oil
3 14-oz cans (3 x 410g tins) whole peeled
  tomatoes, chopped with liquid
½ cup (125ml) freshly chopped basil
Salt and pepper to taste
3 Tbs (45ml) sugar or 4 tsps (20ml) sweetener

Boil pasta for approx. 8–10 mins. Drain with cold water and set aside.

Lightly sauté onion, garlic, and chili paste in olive oil until golden. Add whole peeled tomatoes.

Allow to simmer for at least 45 mins to 1 hour without lid on the pot, so that the sauce thickens, stirring frequently. When thick add freshly chopped basil, salt, pepper and sugar to taste.

NOTE: Pasta can be boiled ahead of time and then rinsed with cold water to stop the cooking process. Just before serving, plunge pasta into boiling water for a few seconds to reheat. Reheat sauce. Toss pasta with a little olive oil to coat. Mix pasta with sauce and serve immediately topped with freshly chopped parsley.

SERVES: 4

Mushroom, asparagus & corn fettucine

Tomato and mozzarella shell pasta

## ROASTED PUMPKIN & MASCARPONE CROOKED PASTA

*When pumpkin is roasted it becomes sweet. I can't begin to describe what that sweetness, the pine nuts, the sage, the ricotta and the mascarpone all do to each other in this amazing taste sensation.*

8 oz (250g) crooked pasta, pipe rigate
2 cups (500ml) very small cubed pumpkin
½ cup (125ml) toasted pine nuts
⅓ cup (80ml) olive oil
⅓ cup (80ml) sage, chopped
1 cup (250ml) chunks of ricotta
1 cup (250ml) mascarpone

Preheat oven to 425 F (220 C).

Place pumpkin cubes in a roasting pan. Drizzle with a little olive oil and season with salt and pepper. Roast and shake the pan until pumpkin is golden.

Cook pasta until soft. Drain.

Toss pasta with toasted pine nuts and ricotta, mascarpone, sage, olive oil and pumpkin cubes.

Season very well with salt and pepper. Sprinkle with a little parmesan for taste if desired. Serve immediately.

SERVES: 4–6

NOTE: Pumpkin can be roasted the day before and reheated. Be careful not to allow it to become too soft. The nuts can be toasted ahead on a baking sheet in a 300 F (140 C) oven until golden.

## SPINACH AND RICOTTA GNOCCHI

*I have made this recipe for years, and it is always the hit of the party. It is so easy to make and can be made a day or two ahead. Bake just before serving and you will see how your guests will rave.*

1 Tbs (15ml) finely chopped onion
2 Tbs (30ml) butter
4½ oz (150g) fresh spinach, spine removed, chopped finely
Salt
¾ cup (175ml) ricotta or cottage cheese
⅔ cup (160ml) flour
2 egg yolks
1 cup (250ml) parmesan cheese
Nutmeg
Salt and pepper to taste

Sauté onion with butter until pale and gold.
Add spinach and a little salt and sauté for 5 mins stirring frequently.

Transfer to mixing bowl. Add ricotta cheese and flour and mix with a spoon. Add egg yolks, parmesan cheese and nutmeg and mix thoroughly. Taste for seasoning.

Bring a large pot of water to boil. Add a little salt. Take ¼ mixture and roll into a sausage on some plastic wrap. Continue making sausages until all the mixture has been used. Place sausage rolls in the refrigerator for 30 mins to set. When cold, peel off plastic wrap and cut into little knuckle-size pieces. Dip knife into flour if necessary to prevent sticking.

Drop gnocchi in water a few at a time. When they float to the surface they are ready. Remove with a slotted spoon. Place in a sprayed ovenproof dish.

### BECHAMEL SAUCE
1½ Tbs (22.5ml) butter
2 cups (500ml) milk
¾ cup (175ml) cream
3 Tbs (45ml) grated emmentaler cheese
(or Swiss or Gruyère cheese)

3 Tbs (45ml) grated parmesan
2½ Tbs (37.5ml) flour
Salt and ground pepper

Melt butter in a pot. Stir in flour and allow to cook for 1 min. Add a little salt and pepper. Turn stove to medium-low and whisk in milk until mixture thickens. Then add cream. Whisk for a few minutes. Remove from heat and stir in emmentaler (or Swiss or Gruyère) and parmesan.

Preheat oven to 375 F (180 C).

Pour sauce over gnocchi. Sprinkle with a little parmesan and bake uncovered on middle rack of oven for 30 to 40 mins or until bubbling.

SERVES: 8–10

## TOMATO & MOZZARELLA SHELL PASTA

If you have access to roma tomatoes, you cannot believe what a wonderful pasta sauce they make. This pasta is sensational, because the hot pasta melts the mozzarella and the colors from the tomatoes are stunning. Make this as soon as you have a chance.

8 oz (250g) large shell pasta
  (conchiglie rigate)
8 oz (250g) ball buffalo mozzarella
  (if available—or other very soft mozzarella
  balls), broken into small pieces
14 oz (400g) baby roma tomatoes
4 large scallions, sliced
  (or baby leeks)
1 Tbs (15ml) dry marjoram
1 Tbs (15ml) dry thyme
1 Tbs (15ml) sugar
¼ cup (60ml) olive oil
Salt and pepper
1¾ oz (50g) arugula (rocket), shredded

Cut tomatoes in half and place in a large frying pan with scallions and olive oil. Sauté on medium heat until they begin to soften. Then add herbs and seasoning and continue to cook until tomatoes are very soft. You will need lots of salt and pepper for taste.

Cook pasta in salty water and toss with a drop of oil after draining.

Toss pasta with sauce, mozzarella pieces, arugula and sprinkle with black pepper. Serve immediately as the mozzarella must be melting with the pasta and tomato sauce as you serve it.

SERVES: 4–6

Sweet and sour beef stir-fry

BEEF & FRIED RICE NOODLES

CHINESE STYLE LAMB

# MEAT

HERB GRILLED RACK OF LAMB

ROAST BEEF WITH MERLOT SAUCE

Whether it's beef, lamb or veal, meat is always a favorite dish. The most important factor to remember when cooking meat is that the longer it is cooked, the tougher it becomes. A good guideline for cooking roasts is:

15 to 20 mins per 1 lb (500g) — medium rare
20 to 25 mins per 1 lb (500g) — medium
25 to 30 mins per 1 lb (500g) — well done

When cooking a sauce for a roast, using alcohol, you need to cook away the pure alcohol taste by boiling the liquid, uncovered, on high for 2 to 3 minutes. This is known as "deglazing."

"Reducing a sauce," on the other hand, means boiling the sauce, uncovered, on medium-high heat to reduce the liquid content, while intensifying the taste.

In the stir-fry recipes, it is important to sear the meat on a very high heat in order to seal in the juices. This must, however, be done in batches to avoid stewing the meat.

# MEAT

BEEF & FRIED RICE NOODLES

BRAISED LAMB SHANK CASSEROLE

CHINESE STYLE LAMB

HERB GRILLED RACK OF LAMB

KOREAN BARBECUED BEEF OR LAMB RIBS

ROAST FILLET WITH GREEN PEPPERCORN SAUCE

ROAST SIRLOIN STEAK WITH MUSHROOMS

ROAST BEEF WITH MERLOT SAUCE

ROAST VEAL WITH TOMATO & WINE

SLOW ROASTED LAMB IN RICH MISO SAUCE

SOY GLAZED RACK OF LAMB

SWEET AND SOUR BEEF STIR-FRY

## BEEF & FRIED RICE NOODLES

This makes a very filling dish that is a meal in itself. Rice noodles are extremely light in texture and make this dish a delight to cook. Should you not be able to use rice noodles, then the lightest, thinnest egg noodles that are available will be quite suitable. You would only need to boil the egg noodles and not soak them. Just toss them in at the end of the cooking.

5 oz (150g) flat rice noodles

Place rice noodles in a bowl of warm water. Allow to soak for 45 mins. Drain when softened.

1 onion, sliced thinly

½ cup (125ml) julienned carrots

6-8 mushrooms, sliced

½ red pepper, sliced thinly

1½ oz (50g) snow peas (mangetouts), cut in half

1½ oz (50g) baby corn, cut in half

3 Tbs (45ml) olive oil

¼ to ½ cup (60 to 125ml) cold water

1 cup (250ml) bean sprouts

3 Tbs (45ml) freshly chopped cilantro

2 Tbs (30ml) chopped toasted peanuts

1 lb (500g) rump steak or any good quality roast, cut into very thin strips

Place meat in a mixing bowl. Toss with 2 to 3 Tbs (10 to 15ml) olive oil, salt and pepper.

Heat a wok until smoking. Add meat in batches and stir-fry until just under cooked. Do not toss too often, sear to seal in juices. Set each batch aside. When all meat is done, keep on the side in a bowl.

Stir fry onion and ginger with a little olive oil until browned. Add carrots and mushrooms. Cook for 2 mins. Then add red pepper, snow peas, and baby corn. Set vegetables aside with meat.

Add rice noodles to wok with the cold water. Allow to cook until water has evaporated, stir-frying all the time.

## SAUCE

1 Tbs (15ml) fresh ginger, very finely chopped

¼ tsp (1.5ml) chili paste or chili powder

2 Tbs (30ml) soy sauce

2 to 3 Tbs (30 to 45ml) hot water

2 Tbs (30ml) sugar

Mix ginger, chili paste, soy, hot water, and sugar together and place in wok with noodles. Bring to a boil and allow to boil rapidly until reduced slightly. Lastly add meat and vegs back in wok, including sprouts, cilantro and peanuts and continue tossing until coated with the sauce.

Serve immediately.

SERVES: 6–8

Beef & fried rice noodles

## BRAISED LAMB SHANK CASSEROLE

The lamb is so tender and succulent that it falls off the bone. This dish is one of our family's favorites because it is so tasty and can be prepared well in advance. It reheats wonderfully if it has been frozen. When you order the meat, ensure that the shanks are cut in large pieces; otherwise the meat will fall off the bone too early.

6 whole lamb shanks, bone broken into thick
  pieces, approx. 2 inches (4cm)
½ cup (125ml) olive oil
½ cup (125ml) dry white wine
Salt and black pepper

Marinate lamb overnight in olive oil, white wine, salt and pepper.

2 Tbs (30ml) olive oil
2 onions, coarsely diced
1 to 2 tsps (5 to 10ml) minced garlic
2 large carrots, coarsely diced
¾ cup (175ml) red wine
1 cup (250ml) beef stock
  (1 Knorr or 2 Telma cubes)
3 to 4 Tbs (45 to 60ml) freshly chopped herbs
  (thyme, rosemary, basil)
14-oz can (410g tin) whole peeled tomatoes,
  chopped with liquid

Heat olive oil in a heavy bottom pot. Sauté onion, garlic and carrot and set aside. Pat shanks dry, season and brown well on all sides. Pour off most of oil when finished. Set aside.

In same pot on high heat, boil down the red wine uncovered for 3 mins to reduce it. Then add stock and continue boiling. Add tomatoes and herbs. Place shanks back in pot with onions and garlic. Cover with lid.

Reduce heat to medium and cook for 3 hours or until shanks are very soft. (You might need to add some extra stock should you use this method as more liquid evaporates with "direct cooking.")

ALTERNATIVE COOKING METHOD:
After putting tomatoes, herbs and shanks in pot, place all ingredients in a casserole, covered with a lid or foil and place on middle rack of 350 F (160 C) oven for 3 hours or until soft.

Vegetables such as baby carrots, potatoes and mushrooms can be added 45 mins before end of cooking time.

NOTE: Can be frozen without vegetables. Can be made a few days ahead and kept in refrigerator.

SERVES: 4–6

## CHINESE STYLE LAMB

The meat takes on a very special flavor when coated with this sauce. It is so tender and can be sliced ahead of time and placed on a serving platter. If you are a lamb lover, then this will become a firm favorite of yours. I like to cook lamb very slowly for a very long time, in the traditional Greek fashion, rather than for a short time where the meat is still a little bit pink.

4 lb (2kg) leg of lamb, or 1 shoulder of lamb
1 cup (250ml) beef stock

### MARINADE
1½ Tbs (20ml) minced garlic
2 Tbs (30ml) sugar
2 Tbs (30ml) freshly chopped ginger
¼ cup (60ml) tomato sauce
4 Tbs (60ml) dark soy sauce
4 Tbs (60ml) medium cream sherry
⅓ cup (80ml) hoisin sauce
  (or other sweet BBQ sauce)
2 Tbs (30ml) honey
2 tsps (10ml) Chinese 5-spice powder

Preheat oven to 350 F (160 C).

Season meat with salt and freshly ground black pepper and pour over the beef stock. Roast covered with foil on middle rack of oven for 2 hours. Uncover and pour half the marinade over 1 side of meat. Raise heat to 375 F (180 C).

Roast for 30 mins, basting several times with more marinade. Turn over and baste other side another 30 mins uncovered. Cover and add extra water if marinade evaporates and meat becomes dry. Allow meat to rest 10 mins before carving.

HANDY TIP: Allow 8 oz (200 to 250g) per person per serving of meat off the bone. If you allow the meat to cool before carving, your slices will be much thinner.

SERVES: 8–10

Roast fillet with green peppercorn sauce

## HERB GRILLED RACK OF LAMB

The combination of flavors from the different herbs gives the meat a sensational taste. The meat takes very little time to cook, and marinating can be done the day before. Allow at least 3 to 4 chops per person. I like them with as little fat as possible.

2 racks of lamb (approx. 9 chops each),
   trimmed of most fat

4 oz (125g) margarine or butter
½ cup (125ml) mint jelly
½ cup (125ml) fresh mint, chopped
½ cup (125ml) fresh herbs (rosemary and
   basil), chopped
3 Tbs (45ml) Lawry's Original Seasoning Salt
   or other seasoning salt
Coarsely ground sea salt
Freshly ground black pepper

Soften margarine or butter and make a paste of all the ingredients. Coat the racks liberally at least 24 hours ahead of time.

Place in an open roasting pan. Grill for 20 mins on each side in middle of the oven until crisp and browned.

Alternatively, racks can be placed on a medium-hot barbecue fire and grilled on each side until nicely browned. Do not allow to burn. Baste frequently.

Serve 3 to 4 chops each.

HANDY TIP: Always leave oven door slightly ajar when grilling to allow element to remain red.

## KOREAN BARBECUED BEEF OR LAMB RIBS

I find that ribs that are boiled before they are marinated are so tender. This also allows you to cut off additional fat. Always choose the least fatty ribs. This sauce is wonderful with either beef or lamb, but make extra ribs, because they're bound to vanish.

2 lb (1 kg) flat beef or lamb ribs

### MARINADE

1 cup (250ml) soy sauce
¼ cup (60ml) rice vinegar*
3 Tbs (45ml) sugar
2 tsps (10ml) minced garlic
1 Tbs (15ml) freshly chopped ginger
   [or 2 tsps (10ml) bottled ginger]
2 Tbs (30ml) sesame oil
1 tsp (5ml) chili sauce (optional)
2 tsps (10ml) sesame seeds

Preheat oven to 400 F (200 C).

Remove most of the fat from the ribs. Place ribs in a pot of cold water and bring to a boil. Boil for 30 minutes. Drain water.

Pour over marinade and place ribs in a roasting pan. Marinade 24 hours ahead if possible.

Cook ribs uncovered for 30 minutes turning to coat until well browned.

Then turn on grill and brown both sides until golden to finish off before serving.

SERVES: 6–8

*See substitutes

## ROAST TENDERLOIN WITH GREEN PEPPERCORN SAUCE

Of all my recipes, this one remains an all-time favorite of mine. The combination between the fillet and the peppercorn sauce is just sensational. Remember not to overcook tenderloin. It is a thin piece of meat and therefore requires very little cooking time.

2½ lb (1 x 1.5kg) tenderloin
1 cup (250ml) soy sauce
¼ cup (60ml) brandy
¼ cup (60ml) red wine

Place meat in marinade overnight seasoning only with ground black pepper, no salt. Turn once during marinating.

Preheat oven to 425 F (220 C). Season meat with garlic salt and additional pepper. Place on bottom rack of oven and roast for 10 mins.

Then turn on grill and move roasting pan up in oven. Grill for a further 10 mins each side until nicely browned.

Fillet should not be cooked longer than 30 mins for 2½ lb (1.5 kg). It should always be served rare in the middle and medium on the outside.

Allow meat to stand for 10 mins before carving.

## PEPPERCORN SAUCE

1 small onion, finely chopped
3 Tbs (45ml) butter or margarine, melted
3 Tbs (45ml) flour
2 Tbs (30ml) brandy
1½ cups (375ml) beef stock
  (1 Knorr or 2 Telma cubes)
2 Tbs (30ml) green peppercorns, crushed
2 Tbs (30ml) liquid from peppercorn bottle
½ cup (125ml) cream or nondairy cream

In a medium-sized pot sauté onion in butter until softened. Stir in flour and cook for 1 min. Add brandy and reduce slightly on high heat. Then add stock, peppercorns and liquid. Allow to thicken and reduce slightly by boiling on medium-heat with lid off for 5 to 8 mins. Add cream and reduce stove to medium. Simmer with lid off until sauce thickens for approximately 15 to 20 mins.

Sauce can be made the day before and reheated.

SERVES: 8–10

# ROAST SIRLOIN STEAK W/MUSHROOMS

I have used a sirloin roast for this dish, but you can use any good quality roast such as fillet or rump. Because sirloin is flat it will not require much cooking time. The meat becomes very tender when it marinates, and the mushroom sauce is delicious with it.

4 lb (2kg) sirloin roast

2 onions, chopped
⅓ cup (80ml) balsamic vinegar
¼ cup (60ml) soy sauce
¼ cup (60ml) sugar

Preheat oven to 425 F (220 C).

Mix onion, balsamic, soy & sugar together and pour over meat. Allow to marinade for at least 24 hours. Turn meat over once during 24 hours.

Cook meat on bottom rack of oven for 15 minutes. Then turn on grill and move meat to middle of oven and grill on each side for 15 minutes. Be careful not to burn the meat. Allow to rest for 10 mins before carving.

NOTE: For Scotch fillet, you will need to cook the meat for a total cooking time of 1½ to 2 hours.

## MUSHROOM SAUCE

1 lb (500g) medium brown mushrooms
¼ lb (125g) porcini mushrooms
  (fresh or dried)
1 onion, thinly sliced
3 Tbs (45ml) olive oil
4 scallions, chopped with green
½ cup (125ml) balsamic vinegar
5 Tbs (75ml) soy sauce
¼ cup (60ml) sugar

Sauté onion in olive oil until softened. Add mushrooms (brown and porcini) and sauté until softened. Add scallions, balsamic vinegar, soy sauce and sugar and bring to a boil. Reduce slightly and adjust seasoning. Set aside.

NOTE: Sauce can be made a few days ahead of time and refrigerated. Reheat on low. Dried porcini mushrooms must be soaked in boiling water for at least 20 to 30 mins to soften them. Drain water before using mushrooms.

SERVES: 10–12

## ROAST BEEF WITH MERLOT SAUCE

The taste of the meat is complemented by this elegant sauce. I like to cook a roast on a very high temperature for a short time, because the outside becomes beautifully browned. There is a richness in the sauce which enhances the taste of the meat. You may substitute tenderloin for any other suitable roast.

4 lb (2kg) tenderloin or beef eye round roast

### MERLOT SAUCE

2 Tbs (15ml) olive oil
⅓ cup (80ml) water
⅓ cup (80ml) sugar
5 Tbs (75ml) red wine vinegar
1 cup (250ml) chopped onion
2½ cups (625ml) merlot or other dry red wine
2 cups (500ml) rich beef stock
  (2 Knorr or 4 Telma cubes)
2 Tbs (30ml) cornstarch (maizena),
  dissolved in ¼ cup cold water

Bring water and sugar to a boil and stir until sugar is dissolved. Boil until light golden in color. Remove from heat and stir in vinegar.

Cook onions in olive oil until softened. Add wine and boil on high heat until reduced by half. Then add stock and continue to boil for about 20 mins. or until greatly reduced. Thicken with cornstarch if necessary.

Lastly place sugar, water and vinegar mixture back in pot. Strain sauce if desired.

### TO COOK MEAT:
Preheat oven to 425 F (220 C).

Season meat very well on outside with salt and pepper. Roast for 15 minutes each side if doing a fillet. If doing any other large roast, cook for approximately 1½ hours until meat is pink inside.

SERVES: 10–12

## ROAST VEAL WITH TOMATO & WINE

Veal is a dish that requires a long cooking process to become tender. Because the meat has a distinct taste, this sauce will bring out the best flavor. It makes a wonderful tender roast.

4 lb (2kg) shoulder or leg of veal
2 1¾-oz (2 x 45g) packets dry brown
  onion soup mix
1 cup (250ml) sweet red wine
  (or kiddush wine)
½ cup (125ml) bottled or fresh lemon juice
6 cups (1+1/2 Litres) water
14-oz can (410g tin) whole peeled tomatoes,
  with liquid
6 sprigs fresh rosemary, chopped
2 to 3 Tbs (30 to 45ml) fresh thyme, chopped

Lightly rub a little olive oil over meat.
Mix ¼ to ½ cup (60ml to 125ml) flour with 1 tsp (5ml) ginger and 1 tsp (5ml) salt. Rub flour mixture all over roast. Place roast in sprayed roasting pan.

Preheat oven to 375 F (180 C). Roast uncovered for 1 hour.

Mix all sauce ingredients together. Pour over meat. Roast covered for another 2 hours, turning meat over halfway through cooking. Uncover to brown meat for 20 to 30 minutes just before serving.

Slice meat thinly and place back in gravy before serving.

NOTE: This roast can be made ahead of time, sliced and placed in the sauce and reheated very successfully.

SERVES: 10–12

Korean barbecued beef or lamb ribs

Roast sirloin steak with mushrooms

Slow roasted lamb in rich miso sauce

## SLOW ROASTED LAMB IN RICH MISO SAUCE

The succulence of the lamb is enhanced by the richness of this sauce. The beauty of this dish is that it cooks very slowly and softens as it cooks. It can be sliced and placed back in the sauce before serving and the meat will become even more tender.

4 lb (2kg) leg or shoulder of lamb
1 cup (250ml) beef stock
  (½ Knorr or 1 Telma cube)

### SAUCE

2 cups (500ml) water
5 oz (140g) Japanese yellow miso paste
2 Tbs (30ml) soy sauce
4 Tbs (60ml) mirin (or sweet rice wine)

Mix all sauce ingredients together.

### VEGETABLES

1 onion, sliced
10 baby potatoes with skin, whole
4 carrots, sliced thickly

Preheat oven to 350 F (160 C).

Place lamb in a roasting pan. Season well with salt and pepper. Pour over beef stock. Cover roasting pan with foil and roast lamb on bottom rack of oven for 2 hours.

Uncover and then pour over miso mixture. Add vegetables and continue roasting uncovered for a further 30 mins each side until golden or until roast is tender. Baste continuously while cooking.

Slice just before serving and place sliced meat in sauce on a serving dish with vegetables around.

NOTE: Lamb can be precooked the day before and warmed, covered with foil, at 300 F (140 C) for 35 to 40 mins. Add water if it is too salty.

SERVES: 10–12

## SOY GLAZED RACK OF LAMB

These racks emerge out of the oven a beautiful color. You can sprinkle them with a few toasted sesame seeds for a final touch. Be careful not to overcook the lamb, it should be slightly pink inside when it is finished cooking.

4 racks of lamb with approx. 6 to 8 chops
  per rack

¾ cup (175ml) water
6 Tbs (90ml) hoisin sauce*
2 Tbs (30ml) beef stock
3 Tbs (45ml) soy sauce
3 Tbs (45ml) medium cream sherry
2 Tbs (30ml) oil
1 tsp (5ml) minced garlic
¼ cup (60ml) rice vinegar**
3 Tbs (45ml) dijon mustard

Whisk all ingredients together.

Preheat oven to 425 F (220 C). Season racks with any seasoning salt and pepper. Place in a roasting pan and roast 20 mins.

Brush sauce all over the racks and turn on grill. Grill on all sides for a further 10 mins each side until browned.

Serve 3 to 4 chops per person.

SERVES: 8–10

* sweet barbeque sauce
**see substitutes

Herb grilled rack of lamb

# SWEET AND SOUR BEEF STIR-FRY

The colors of the vegetables make this a great quick and easy stir-fry. It is most delicious when done with a very good quality meat like rump or fillet, as the meat remains tender. If you coat your meat with a little oil before stir-frying, this eliminates the necessity of adding oil to the wok.

2 lbs (1kg) good quality steak (rump)
  or a tender roast, cut into strips
1 Tbs (15ml) olive oil
1 Tbs (15ml) minced garlic
1 red pepper, cut into triangles
1 yellow pepper, cut into triangles
2 carrots, julienned
¼ cup (100g) snow peas (mangetouts)

## SAUCE
½ cup (125ml) tomato sauce
1 to 2 Tbs (15 to 30ml) dark soy sauce
2 tsps (10ml) salt
1 Tbs (15ml) Worcestershire sauce
2 Tbs (30ml) sugar
1 Tbs (15ml) oil
½ cup (125ml) chicken stock
  (1 Knorr or 1 Telma cube)
2 to 3 Tbs (30 to 45ml) cornstarch (maizena),
  dissolved in ⅓ cup cold water (to thicken
  sauce)

Heat a wok on high until almost smoking.

Place meat in a bowl and coat with 2 Tbs (30ml) olive oil. Season with salt and pepper.

When wok is very hot, stir-fry meat in batches, searing on one side and then quickly turning and searing other side. Set aside. Do not overcook, as meat will toughen.

Heat garlic in olive oil. Add carrots, peppers and snowpeas. Stir-fry for 3 mins and then set aside with meat.

Mix all sauce ingredients together and bring to a boil. Thicken with cornstarch. Sauce should be a little too thick in order to coat the meat well.

Place meat and vegetables back in wok. Cook for 1 minute to coat. Remove from heat. Serve with rice or noodles.

HANDY TIP: This dish can be reheated in the microwave for 5 to 8 mins, stirred and then heated again for another 5 to 8 mins. If planning to reheat, do not add snowpeas to the vegetables when stir-frying initially as they will overcook. Add them only when reheating.

SERVES: 4–6

Braised lamb shank casserole

Roast veal with tomato and wine

Egg noodles with vegetables and chicken

CHICKEN WELLINGTON

ORIENTAL CHICKEN PIECES

# POULTRY

DUCK WITH CHERRIES

THAI RED CHICKEN CURRY

Poultry, for me, is an easy, low-fat, versatile food that is great for everyday meals or as an elegant dinner-party dish.

The trick to succulent chicken is not to overcook it. Here are some guidelines which I believe will help you with your cooking times:

BONELESS AND SKINLESS BREASTS—20 MINS
BREASTS WITH SKIN AND BONE—30 MINS
CHICKEN PIECES—45 MINS
WHOLE CHICKEN—90 MINS

If you follow these cooking times you will never have dried out chicken. Remember that sweet marinades and sauces burn under the broiler, so be careful not to place the food too close to the broiler.

Whenever I broil, I use the highest setting on the broiler. I never change that. I then adjust the racks of the oven either up or down. Always leave your oven door slightly open so that the element remains red. This ensures that the food broils.

You have to use common sense as well, because if something is burning but not cooked properly, you will need to turn off the broiler but leave the oven on a high temperature until the food is cooked through.

As much as we like to cook food before our guests arrive, there are some foods that need to come out of the oven straight to the table. Quite honestly, there is nothing nicer than a succulent, juicy chicken breast that has not been overcooked.

# POULTRY

CHICKEN LASAGNE

CHICKEN WELLINGTON

CHICKEN WITH FRIED NOODLE PANCAKE

DUCK WITH CHERRIES

EGG NOODLES WITH VEGETABLES AND CHICKEN

GRILLED CHICKEN BREASTS STUFFED WITH CORN

LEMON & HERB GRILLED CHICKEN

ORIENTAL CHICKEN PIECES

PAAD THAI NOODLES

THAI RED CHICKEN CURRY

WHOLE ROASTED CHICKEN WITH VEGETABLES

YUMMY CHICKEN PIE

# CHICKEN LASAGNE

I love making this dish because it can be prepared ahead of time and baked just before you eat. It is very tasty and makes a nice change from the usual meat lasagne. To ensure that the lasagne sheets are not hard, you must allow the lasagne to stand for a few hours to absorb the liquid and to soften before baking.

8 oz (250g) "no cooking required" green
   lasagne sheets (12 sheets)
2 lbs (1 kg) skinless and boneless chicken,
   cut into strips
3 large onions, coarsely chopped
1 tsp (5ml) minced garlic
¼ cup (60ml) oil
¼ cup (60ml) chopped parsley
8 oz (250g) white mushrooms, sliced
14-oz can (410g tin) whole peeled tomatoes,
   chopped with juice
7½-oz can (225g tin) tomato purée
3 bay leaves
½ cup (125ml) water

Sauté onion and garlic in oil until golden. Add chicken and sauté. Add parsley, mushrooms, tomatoes, tomato purée, seasoning, bay leaves, water and a little sugar. Simmer for a few minutes or until chicken is soft. Set aside.

## SAUCE

1 - 2 onions, chopped
6 Tbs (90ml) butter or margarine
¼ cup (60ml) flour
3 cups (750ml) chicken stock
   (1.5 Knorr or 3 Telma cubes)
4 egg yolks
2 Tbs (30ml) cream or nondairy creamer

Sauté onions in butter or margarine until golden. Add flour and cook for 1 min over medium heat.

Add chicken stock and whisk to make a smooth sauce. Remove from heat and quickly whisk beaten egg yolks into half the sauce. Then add this to the other half of the sauce. Add nondairy creamer or cream (if desired) to make it a little creamy. Set aside.

In a large ovenproof dish, first layer half the chicken mixture, then some lasagne sheets (do not overlap sheets), then half sauce, more lasagne, remainder of chicken, finishing with sauce. Make sure all sheets are covered. Sprinkle with breadcrumbs.

Preheat oven to 375 F (180 C). Bake for 60 to 90 mins uncovered in middle of oven until bubbling and golden or until soft when pricked in middle with a fork.

NOTE: Can be made ahead and placed covered in refrigerator overnight. Can be frozen, then defrosted in refrigerator overnight and baked as above.

SERVES: 10–12

Chicken with fried noodle pancake

# CHICKEN WELLINGTON

*If you really want to impress your guests, make this easy-to-prepare dish ahead of time. Do not cook it until you are about to eat, because the chicken will be dry. The sauce can also be prepared a day or two ahead of time. It is better to bake it directly on the serving platter or dish so that it cuts very easily.*

6 boneless and skinless chicken breasts

8 oz (2 x 250g) medium brown mushrooms, chopped

4 leeks, sliced and chopped, white part only

4 Tbs (60ml) olive oil

Salt and freshly ground black pepper

14 oz (400g) packet puff pastry

1 egg beaten with 1 Tsp (15ml) water

Sauté leeks and mushrooms in olive oil until very soft. Season with salt and pepper.

Grease an ovenproof dish.

Slit each chicken breast at thick end to make a little pocket. Stuff with mushroom mixture. Place breasts in a line overlapping each other. Top with remaining mushroom-leek mixture.

Roll out puff pastry and cover entire chicken mixture with pastry. Brush with egg glaze.
Using extra puff pastry cut a long strip to fit length of puff pastry. Tuck under and then twist to make a long strip over the top of the wellington for decoration. Tuck under the other side. Brush strip with egg. Preheat oven to 425 F (220 C). Bake for 20 to 25 mins. Serve immediately with sauce on side.

## SAUCE

2 Tbs (30ml) olive oil

1 small onion, finely chopped

2 Tbs (30ml) flour

2 cups (500ml) mushrooms, sliced

½ cup (125ml) brandy

½ cup (125ml) medium cream sherry or sweet white wine

1 cup (250ml) chicken stock
  (1 Knorr or 2 Telma cubes)

½ cup (125ml) cream

1 tsp (5ml) paprika

Sauté onion in olive oil. Add mushrooms and cook for a few mins.
Stir in flour. Deglaze with brandy and sherry or wine and boil down for a few mins.
Add chicken stock. Allow to reduce for 3 mins.
Add cream, paprika and pepper. Reduce until thickened. Season to taste.

NOTE: The breasts can be stuffed and covered with the pastry. Place in the refrigerator and cover with plastic wrap the day before serving. It is preferable to bring them to room temperature before baking.

# CHICKEN WITH FRIED NOODLE PANCAKE

*What a way to wow a crowd! The breasts look magnificent on the crispy noodle pancake topped with very thinly julienned vegetables and drizzled with sauce. They have an oriental look and taste, and the crunchiness of the noodles complements the softness of the vegetables and the chicken. I have often half-cooked the breasts and then placed them under the broiler to finish them off.*

6 chicken breasts, bone removed, skin on

## MARINADE

2 tsps (10ml) minced garlic

4 Tbs (60ml) bottled lemon juice

2 Tbs (30ml) chutney
  (or other sweet chunky relish)

1 cup (250ml) chicken stock
  (½ Knorr or 1 Telma cube)

1 red pepper, cut into thin strips

1 yellow pepper, cut into thin strips

1 stick celery, cut into thin strips,
  about 2 inches (4 cm) long

1 carrot, julienned (cut into shorter lengths)

2 Tbs (30ml) thick soy sauce
2 Tbs (30ml) smooth peanut butter
2 Tbs (30ml) apricot jam diluted until runny
  with boiling water
8 oz (250g) packet thin Chinese egg noodles

Marinate chicken breasts in garlic, lemon juice,
chutney, salt and pepper for 30 mins.

Drain marinade and place marinade with the
chicken stock in a wok and allow to reduce on
high heat until slightly thickened approx 7-8 mins.
Set aside.

In the same wok, or on a separate grilling pan,
grill breasts on each side for 8 mins or until golden.
Reduce heat as necessary so they don't burn. Make
2 big slits in each breast to ensure they are
cooked. Keep warm in a 325 F (140 C) oven.

Reheat wok until very hot. Place reduced chicken
stock sauce, soy sauce, peanut butter and apricot
jam in wok and reduce on high until very thick.
Add vegetables and only cook long enough to wilt
them (6 mins).

NOODLES: Boil egg noodles for 5 mins as directed
and then rinse with cold water. Dry very well. Heat
some oil in a frying pan and make small handfuls
of noodles. Fry on high heat in batches until very
brown and very crisp. Place on paper towel to
drain after frying.

NOTE: Noodles can be made several days in
advance and kept in a Tupperware until ready to
use. They do not need to be reheated. Vegetables
can be julienned the day before.

TO SERVE: Place a noodle pancake on each plate.
Top with chicken breast, spoon some vegetables and
sauce over each breast. Serve immediately.

SERVES: 6

# DUCK WITH CHERRIES

If you are a duck lover, this is a wonderfully tasty addition to
your repertoire. The duck must be cooked first without any sauce
to allow the fat to drain off. When it is really crispy, pour over
the sauce and continue to cook.

1 whole duck

1 Tbs (15ml) corn syrup
Juice and rind of 1 orange
1 tsp (5ml) ground ginger
1 Tbs (15ml) soy sauce
1 Tbs (15ml) fresh lemon juice
14-oz (410g) can pitted black cherries,
  drained; reserve ½ can of juice
1 Tbs (15ml) cornstarch (maizena), dissolved
  in 1 Tbs cold water

Preheat oven to 400 F (200 C).

Place duck on a rack in a roasting pan to allow fat
to drip off. Season with salt and pepper. Prick all
over with a fork. Roast uncovered for 2 hours until
very crispy and brown, turning to brown all sides.
Pour off all fat and oil but keep remaining gravy.

Bring sauce ingredients to a boil. Thicken with
cornstarch. Allow to thicken until it coats a spoon.
Add reserved duck gravy. Allow to boil gently
without the lid for 5 to 8 mins or until thickened.

Cut up duck and pour sauce over. Place back in
oven to reheat on 375 F (180 C).

SERVES: 4–6

## EGG NOODLES WITH VEGETABLES AND CHICKEN

*My family enjoys an all-in-one type of meal like this. It is quick and easy to prepare and tastes absolutely delicious.*

7 oz (200g) dried egg noodles (very thin)

1 tsp (15ml) sesame oil

1 onion, chopped

⅓ cup (80ml) cold water

1 red pepper, cut into short strips

½ eggplant, skin on, cut into thin strips

1 carrot, julienned

4-6 fresh asparagus, cut into pieces

3 medium baby zucchinis,
  cut into thin short strips

3½ oz (100g) baby corn, cut into thin strips

7 oz (200g) bok choy or tah tsai*, chopped

3 chicken breasts, cut very thin into small strips

3 Tbs (45ml) dark soy sauce

2 Tbs (30ml) mirin (sweet wine)**

¼ cup (60ml) chicken stock
  (½ Knorr or 1 Telma chicken cube)

Boil egg noodles until 'al dente.' Drain and rinse with cold water and allow to cool.

Heat a little oil in a wok and add onion. Cook until golden. Add chicken pieces and stir-fry quickly. Remove from wok and set aside. Add eggplant and a little more oil. Cook eggplant on high heat until quite well done. Then add baby zucchini, carrot, red pepper and corn. Season well with salt and pepper and allow to cook until slightly wilted. Set aside with chicken.

Place soya sauce, mirin and stock in wok and bring to a boil. Allow to bubble until thickened. Then put vegetables and noodles back into wok. Toss with sauce and sauté until heated through. Add bok choy or tah tsai just before serving. Add a little chili if desired.

SERVES: 4–6
\* See substitutes
\*\* See substitutes

## GRILLED CHICKEN BREASTS STUFFED WITH CORN

*Whichever way you make this dish, it is a simple, elegant main course. The chicken breasts can be stuffed with mushrooms or corn. This can be done the day before. Be careful not to over-cook the breasts as they can become very dry. Serve with the potato rosti; your guests will love them.*

8 chicken breasts with skin on, bone removed

14-oz can (410g tin) corn kernels

4 Tbs (60ml) sun-dried tomatoes, finely chopped

2 scallions, thinly sliced

2 Tbs (30ml) freshly chopped cilantro

Salt and pepper

Drain corn kernels and mix with sun-dried tomatoes, scallion, fresh cilantro and season to taste.

Make a slit in the thick side of each chicken breast and stuff with a little corn mixture. Seal with a toothpick.

Season chicken with coarse salt and pepper and brown in a drop of olive oil in a very hot frying pan on both sides for 2 mins.

Set aside on a sprayed baking sheet until all breasts are seared.

Finish baking them for 20 to 25 mins uncovered in a 425 F (220 C) oven.

Drizzle each breast with a little cilantro oil (see index).

SERVES: 6–8

Egg noodles with vegetables and chicken

Grilled chicken breasts stuffed with corn

# LEMON & HERB GRILLED CHICKEN

*This chicken dish will become a firm favorite of yours because it is so tasty and delicious. As long as chicken is not overcooked, it will not be too dry. I like to cut the chicken open so that the inside can be flavored as well.*

3 lbs (1 X 1.5 kg) chicken, split on
  breastbone and opened (butterflied)
Juice of 2 lemons
Freshly ground black pepper

## SEASONING

1 Tbs (15ml) barbeque spice
1 tsp (5ml) garlic salt
1 tsp (5ml) onion salt
1 tsp (5ml) paprika
1 Tbs (15ml) chicken seasoning
1 tsp (5ml) mixed herbs (dry)

Preheat oven to 400 F (200 C). Spray a small roasting pan.

Wash and flatten the chicken and place skin side down on roasting pan. Squeeze lemon juice all over chicken. Mix all seasonings together and liberally sprinkle some over one side of the chicken. Grind a little pepper on top.

Place chicken on bottom rack of oven and roast for 30 mins. Turn chicken over and season other side (you may have some seasoning over) and roast for a further 30 mins.

Pour 1 cup water into roasting pan. Turn chicken to skin side down and now turn broiler on. Place chicken in lower part of oven and broil for approx. 10 to 15 mins. Finish by broiling skin side up for another 10 to 15 mins.

HANDY TIP: A whole chicken will take exactly 90 mins to cook perfectly, i.e., breast will still be juicy and not dry. Prick leg and thigh to see if juices run clear (yellow). This indicates that chicken is cooked.

NOTE: The bigger the roasting pan the more evaporation you have and the more gravy and juices will dry out. Use a smaller roasting pan for only one chicken. Increase your cooking time by 50%, if you have more than one chicken.

SERVES: 4–6

Lemon and herb grilled chicken

## ORIENTAL CHICKEN PIECES

*These tasty and sticky chicken pieces are perfect if you are in a hurry. They look great and go very well with some basmati rice or couscous, a green salad and a vegetable stir-fry. What more could one want?*

10 to 12 drumsticks, wings or thighs

¼ cup (60ml) soy sauce

2 tsps (10ml) minced garlic

1 Tbs (15ml) medium cream sherry (sweet wine)

3 Tbs (45ml) honey or syrup

½ tsp (2.5ml) ground nutmeg

½ tsp (2.5ml) ground ginger

2 tsps (10ml) Peri-Peri oil or hot chili oil

2 Tbs (30ml) sunflower oil

¼ cup (60ml) water

Whisk all ingredients together. Pour sauce over chicken pieces a few hours before cooking and allow to marinate.

Preheat oven to 375 F (180 C). Bake chicken on bottom rack of oven for 40 mins uncovered, turning once during cooking. Then grill on both sides moving roasting pan to middle of the oven for a further 10 mins or until golden.

SERVES: 4–6

## PAAD THAI NOODLES

*My husband's favorite dish. Rice noodles are so light they are like eating air. This is also such a healthy recipe.*

5 oz (150g) thin dried rice noodles

4 Tbs (60ml) oil

2 Tbs (30ml) sugar or palm sugar

1 Tbs (15ml) lime juice

4 Tbs (60ml) soy sauce

1 tsp (5ml) chili paste

1 cup (250ml) bean sprouts

¼ cup (60ml) green stalks from scallion

7 oz (200g) (1 bunch) Chinese spinach (tah tsai)*

1 egg, beaten and fried

4 chicken breasts, cut into very thin strips

¼ to ½ cup (60 to 125ml) water

   (If stir-fry looks dry add the extra water)

Cover rice noodles with warm water and soak for 15 to 20 mins. Mix together the sugar, lime juice, soy sauce, chili paste. Set aside. In a wok fry beaten egg in a drop of oil. Set aside.

Add chicken in batches to wok with a little oil and fry until half cooked. Add noodles and sauce and fry very quickly on high heat, stirring all the time.

Return chicken and egg to wok. Continue stir-frying. Lastly add tah tsai and scallions and fry for 1 min. Sprinkle with bean sprouts and chopped nuts if desired.

SERVES: 4–6

* See substitutes

## THAI RED CHICKEN CURRY

*Red curry paste is more subtle than green and the color is beautiful. I love making this dish because of its simplicity and great taste.*

2 lb (1 kg) boneless and skinless chicken
   breasts, cut into strips

1 Tbs (15ml) olive oil

2 Tbs (30ml) red curry paste

13½ oz (400ml) coconut milk

2 Tbs (30ml) brown sugar

1 Tbs (15ml) soy sauce

¼ cup (60ml) freshly chopped basil leaves

½ to 1 tsp (2.5-5ml) chili paste

1 tsp (5ml) paprika

1 tsp (5ml) cumin

Stir the olive oil into the chicken strips and season with salt and pepper.

Heat a wok, and quickly sear the chicken in batches, undercooking slightly. Set aside. (Too much chicken cooked at one time creates a stewing effect.)

Place curry paste, coconut milk, brown sugar, soy sauce, basil, chili, paprika and cumin in wok and bring to a boil. Reduce heat and allow to simmer until thickened. Place chicken back in wok and cook completely.

Serve with steamed jasmine rice and stir-fried vegetables.

SERVES: 4–6

Paad Thai noodles

Thai red chicken curry

## WHOLE ROAST CHICKEN WITH VEGETABLES

This has to be my daughter's top favorite dish, because it combines all the vegetables as well as the chicken. The veggies absorb the chicken flavor, and the meal requires nothing else but a large salad. It is so tasty and juicy everyone will love it. Just ensure that your veggies fit around the chicken because they take up quite a bit of space.

3 lbs (1.5 kg) chicken, split down breastbone

2 tsps (10ml) coarsely ground sea salt
2 tsps(10ml) seasoning salt
2 tsps (10ml) Herbamare
   (or other seasoning salt)

Freshly ground black pepper

8 oz (250g) peeled baby carrots
3 potatoes, cut into quarters,
   or 8 - 10 baby potatoes with skin
8 oz (250g) baby zucchini (marrows),
   cut into chunks
8 oz (250g) pumpkin or butternut chunks
8 oz (250g) white mushrooms
7 oz (100g) fresh baby corn
2 onions, cut into quarters
2 cups (500ml) boiling water
Sprigs of fresh herbs
   (thyme, parsley, tarragon)

Preheat oven to 400 F (200 C).

Rub seasoning on inside and outside of chicken. Place chicken in pre-sprayed roasting pan on bottom rack of oven. Roast for 30 mins skin side down with no liquid and no vegetables.

Precook potatoes in microwave for 4 mins on high. Turn chicken over with skin side up and place all vegetables except mushrooms around chicken.

Season vegetables with some coarse salt and continue to roast for another 30 mins.

Place sprigs of herbs around chicken and add boiling water and continue to roast skin side up for another 30 mins. Keep basting chicken with juices to enhance flavor. Feel if vegetables are cooked and add extra seasoning to taste, and water if necessary for more gravy.

Chicken needs 90 minutes to be perfectly cooked.

SERVES: 4–6

## YUMMY CHICKEN PIE

There is nothing nicer than a good old-fashioned home-made chicken pie, and this one is really good.

1 whole precooked chicken,
   skin and bones removed
8 oz (250g) white mushrooms, sliced
6 oz (175g) mixed baby zucchinis,
   green and yellow summer squash
3½ oz (100g) baby corn
7 oz (200g) baby carrots
6 oz (175g) snow peas

14 oz (400g) roll puff pastry

**SAUCE**
2 Tbs (30ml) margarine or butter
3 Tbs (45ml) flour
1½ cups (375ml) chicken stock
   (2 Knorr or 3 Telma cubes)
¼ cup (60ml) lemon juice
Rind of 1 lemon

Remove the skin and bones of the chicken, leaving the meat in large chunks. Set aside.

Cook mushrooms on high in a frying pan without oil, season with salt and pepper and fry until there is no liquid left in the pan. Set aside.

Place baby carrots in microwave for 2 to 3 mins to precook them.

Chop baby zucchinis, summer squash, corn and snow peas. Place vegs in frying pan on high and quickly cook them for 2 mins to heat through. Add to mushrooms.

Melt margarine or butter. Add flour and stir in for 1 minute. Slowly whisk in the stock until thickened. Then add lemon juice and lemon rind and season again to taste. Add chicken pieces and make sure sauce covers all chicken. Add vegetables. If too dry, add a little extra boiling water. Allow to cool.

Spray a deep baking dish. Place chicken and vegetable mixture in dish.

Roll out sufficient puff pastry to fit top of dish and cover chicken with a little overhang [approx. ¼ inch (½ cm ) on all sides] to allow pastry to shrink.

Don't press pastry down. Brush with beaten egg mixed with water. Make a hole in the middle.

Bake in the middle of preheated 400 F (200 C) oven for 20 to 25 mins or until golden brown.

NOTE: Can be made ahead and covered with plastic wrap. Place in fridge until ready to bake. Bring to room temperature before baking.

SERVES: 10–12

Whole roast chicken with vegetables

Chicken wellington

Pan roasted vegetables

GRILLED VEGETABLE KEBABS

PAN ROASTED VEGETABLES

# VEGETABLES

VEGETABLE LASAGNE

ROASTED VEGETABLE PLATTER

The days of making separate vegetables are gone. Instead we can now create wonderful, colorful assorted vegetable platters. There is nothing nicer than a colorful assortment of beautifully stir-fried or roasted vegetables.

Vegetable platters are interesting and different and many types of vegetables can be used. Substitute any vegetables that you don't eat with ones that you do in corresponding quantities.

Take advantage of the many prepacked vegetable combinations available which will reduce waste as you can buy smaller quantities. For example, use a mixed pack of snow peas, baby corn, and carrots instead of buying separate packs of each.

Some recipes mention "dry-frying." This means that vegetables like mushrooms, which contain a lot of water, do not need additional oil or other moisture in the pan.

When roasting vegetables, I always do them on very high heat at approximately 450 F (220 C) so that they brown nicely on the bottom. They also absorb a lot of seasoning, so be generous in order to bring out the most intense flavor in them.

# VEGETABLES

ASSORTED VEGETABLES WITH COUSCOUS

BUTTERNUT GNOCCHI WITH PUMPKIN SEEDS & SAGE BUTTER

GRILLED VEGETABLE KEBABS

MEDLEY OF GLAZED BABY VEGETABLES

MIXED STIR-FRIED VEGETABLES

PAN ROASTED VEGETABLES

ROASTED VEGETABLE PLATTER

VEGETABLE LASAGNE

VEGETABLE SPRING ROLLS IN PHYLLO

# ASSORTED VEGETABLES WITH COUSCOUS

If you are a vegetable fan, then this is a marvelous dish because it combines many vegetables and looks spectacular on a bed of couscous. The vegetables can be made ahead of time and undercooked slightly. Reheat in a microwave on high for at least 4 to 5 mins or until heated through.

1 onion, diced

8 oz (250g) mushrooms, whole

8 oz (250g) ready peeled baby carrots

14-oz can (410g tin) baby corn

4 oz (125g) thin green beans

8 oz (250g) pumpkin or butternut,
  peeled and diced

8 oz (250g) snow peas

1 eggplant, diced skin on

8 oz (250g) baby zucchinis, thinly sliced

½ sweet potato (or yam), peeled and diced

8 oz (250g) baby butternut, quartered (if available)

8 oz (250g) small yellow summer squash

Fry onion in a hot wok until golden. Then add mushrooms, seasoning while sautéing them.

Cook hardest vegetables first, i.e. carrots, eggplant, sweet potato, beans and baby butternuts. Then add other vegetables slowly, one at a time ending with snow peas and baby corn. Season vegetables generously with coarse salt, black pepper and Herbamare (if available). Place in a colander and allow excess juices to drain.

## SAUCE

3 Tbs (45ml) soft brown sugar

½ cup (125ml) teriyaki sauce*

1 Tbs (15ml) dark soy sauce

2 Tbs (30ml) balsamic vinegar

1 Tbs (15ml) sweet chili sauce*

* See substitutes

In the same wok, bring all sauce ingredients to a boil and reduce slightly until thickened.

Toss over vegetables just before serving. Reheat vegetables on high in microwave for 5 to 8 mins or until hot.

COUSCOUS: 2 CUPS DRY COUSCOUS—cook according to directions on box. Place heated vegetables on couscous just before serving.

SERVES: 10–15

Assorted vegetables with couscous

## BUTTERNUT GNOCCHI WITH PUMPKIN SEEDS & SAGE BUTTER

*The best thing about this dish is that it looks fantastic and tastes even better. It is wonderful served as a vegetable or with other pastas. If pumpkin seeds are not available, use pine nuts.*

### GNOCCHI

2 cups (500ml) cooked butternut
4 Tbs (90g) melted salted butter
½ cup (125ml) semolina flour
½ cup (125ml) parmesan
3 eggs, beaten
1 tsp (5ml) minced garlic
⅓ cup (80ml) chopped chives
Freshly ground black pepper
Salt

Mix all ingredients for gnocchi in a mixing bowl. Spray a small baking sheet with nonstick spray. Spread mixture onto sheet and smooth out to ¼-inch (1-cm) thickness.

Preheat oven to 375 F (180 C). Bake for 30 mins or until golden and firm to touch. Allow to cool. Loosen in pan and invert on to a board. Cut into diamond shapes with a sharp knife.

### SAGE BUTTER

8 Tbs (125g) salted butter
½ cup (125ml) pumpkin seeds (pepitas)
¼ cup (60ml) chopped fresh sage

Parmesan shavings

BUTTER: Melt butter and allow to brown in a medium frying pan. Add pumpkin seeds and allow them to puff up. Be careful that they do not splatter and pop. Add sage and stir gently. Remove from heat.

Place cut diamond-shaped gnocchi in a sprayed ovenproof dish in overlapping layers in rows. Heat uncovered at 375 F (180 C) oven for approx. 20 to 25 mins. Drizzle with butter, pumpkin seeds and sage. Sprinkle with black pepper and parmesan shavings.

NOTE: Freeze cut diamonds of gnocchi after baking. Defrost and then heat uncovered as directed above.

HANDY TIP: The pumpkin seeds must be peeled. They are usually available at health shops. They are also called "pepitas."

SERVES: 6

## GRILLED VEGETABLE KEBABS

*When you have a barbeque, these look very colorful, in addition to being very yummy. My pet hate is when you pre-buy vegetable kebabs and the vegetables do not all cook at the same time and some of the vegetables are raw and hard. By cooking them this way, they taste and look great.*

3 ears corn on the cob, cut into thick slices
5 baby zucchinis, cut into chunks
1 red pepper, cut into squares
8 oz (250g) mushrooms
12 baby onions
12 pumpkin chunks
½ cup (125ml) honey mustard salad dressing
  (or any creamy salad dressing)

Cook corn on the cob for approx. 10 mins in boiling water.

Blanch baby zucchinis, baby onions and pumpkin pieces for 5 mins in the same water. Drain.

Marinate vegetables in a roasting pan for a few hours with sauce. Then thread on to metal kebab skewers, and season well with seasoning salt and pepper.

Grill on a very hot grilling pan or barbecue, turning continuously until well browned and baste continuously with sauce.

SERVES: 10–12

Butternut gnocchi with pumpkin seed & sage butter

Grilled vegetable kebabs

## MEDLEY OF GLAZED BABY VEGETABLES

*When you blanch vegetables, they are all cooked correctly. The colors make this dish very bright, and each vegetable tastes equally delicious.*

7 oz (200g) peeled baby carrots
3½ oz (100g) snow peas (mangetouts)
8 oz (125g) very thin green beans
8 oz (250g) button mushrooms
7 oz (200g) baby yellow summer squash
½ red pepper, sliced
½ yellow pepper, sliced

3 Tbs (45ml) butter or margarine
1 to 2 tsps (5 to 10ml) sugar or sweetener
Salt and pepper

* Bring a pot of water to a boil. Blanch each vegetable separately in the boiling water and then place immediately into ice water.

Carrots, beans, summer squash—5 mins
Snowpeas, mushrooms—2 mins
Peppers do not need blanching.
[This ensures that each vegetable is perfectly cooked; and also this can be done ahead of time.]

Melt butter or margarine in a wok or large pot. Add vegetables and toss gently including red and yellow pepper. Season with salt, pepper and sugar.

SERVE IMMEDIATELY

NOTE: If you are blanching the vegetables earlier in the day do not toss them with butter or margarine or season them.

Instead place them in the microwave for 5 mins on high to heat, then toss them, add butter or margarine and seasoning and heat again for another 4 mins or until heated through.

When they are heated through completely serve immediately. They will remain crisp and not lose their color.

SERVES: 6

## MIXED STIR-FRIED VEGETABLES

*By cutting each vegetable as instructed, the vegetables all cook together and make a wonderful display, as well as tasting delicious. I love making this stir-fry.*

1 small eggplant, skin on,
  sliced in small strips
8 oz (250g) button mushrooms, quartered
½ red onion, sliced thinly (if available)
4 oz (125g) small baby zucchinis,
  sliced in rounds
7 oz (200g) yellow summer squash, sliced thinly
7 oz (200g) baby butternut, cut in half and
  then sliced (if available)
3½ oz (100g) baby corn, cut in half lengthwise
½ small red pepper, cut into small strips
½ small yellow pepper, cut into small strips
4 oz (125g) very fine green beans, cut in half
4 oz (125g) fresh asparagus, cut into pieces
  (if available)
1½ oz (50g) snow peas,
  cut into smaller strips
2 carrots, julienned

### SEASONING
Coarse salt
Herbamare
Black pepper
Freshly ground herb blend
  (in grinder form if available)
Olive oil or olive oil spray

Heat a wok until very hot. Add a drop of olive oil and fry mushrooms, eggplant and onion until very brown and very dry. Set aside.

Then stir-fry remainder of vegetables except snow peas, asparagus and peppers. Season vegetables very well as you stir-fry with seasoning.
Continue to sauté until vegs are almost cooked through and then add snowpeas and asparagus and peppers. Serve immediately.

SERVES: 8

Medley of glazed baby vegetables

Roasted vegetable platter

## PAN ROASTED VEGETABLES

*If the oven temperature is high enough, your vegetables turn a beautiful golden color. Do not crowd too many vegetables into a roasting pan; rather use two or they won't brown. This is heaven for a vegetarian.*

2 large potatoes, cut into wedges
1 large onion, cut into wedges
1 lb (500g) butternut or pumpkin,
    peeled and cut into chunks
1 lb (500g) carrots, cut into chunks
8 oz (250g) baby zucchinis,
    cut into chunks
4 Tbs (60ml) olive oil
2 tsps (10ml) minced garlic
1 tsp (5ml) mixed herbs
Sprigs of fresh rosemary
Sprigs of fresh thyme
2 bay leaves
Salt and pepper

Arrange the vegetables in a roasting pan. Pour over oil, garlic, mixed herbs, fresh herbs and bay leaves. Season very well with salt and pepper and Herbamare (if available).

Preheat oven to 425 F (220 C). Roast uncovered on bottom rack for at least 1 hour shaking pan to stop vegetables sticking and cook until they are soft.

SERVES: 12–15

## ROASTED VEGETABLE PLATTER

*Vegetables are very tasty when roasted like this. They look great presented in rows on a platter, and make a colorful display. Do not overcook them.*

1 eggplant, sliced with skin on
8 oz (250g) baby zucchinis (marrows), sliced
7 oz (200g) yellow summer squash, sliced
8 oz (250g) medium brown mushrooms
8 oz (250g) very thin green beans
1 whole head garlic
1 head fennel, cut into quarters

½ cup (125ml) chicken stock
    (½ Knorr or 1 Telma cube)
Olive oil
Balsamic vinegar
Salt and pepper

Place vegetables in baking dish in rows, excluding mushrooms and beans. Pour over chicken stock and place in 375 F (180 C) oven for 30 to 40 mins. Season well.

Add beans and mushrooms. Brush vegetables with olive oil and balsamic vinegar and season again.

Continue to roast vegetables until they soften (another 30 mins). Place on a platter and serve.

SERVES: 8–10

## VEGETABLE LASAGNE

*This makes the most marvelous meal for vegetarians, as well as being an all-in-one vegetable dish.*

9½ oz (300g) bunch fresh spinach,
    finely chopped and lightly sautéed to wilt
    (drained well)
1 small eggplant, sliced with skin on
    and cut into cubes
8 oz (250g) fresh button mushrooms, sliced
4 oz (125g) baby zucchinis, sliced
2 Tbs (30ml) olive oil
2 onions, finely chopped
1 tsp (5ml) minced garlic
2 14-oz cans (2 x 410g tins) whole peeled
    Italian tomatoes chopped with liquid
2 tsps (10ml) dry basil
2 tsps (10ml) dry oregano

Sauté onions and garlic in oil until soft. Add eggplant and mushrooms and sauté until some of the liquid has evaporated. Add baby zucchini. Sauté gently.

Add chopped tomatoes, basil, oregano, salt and pepper and 1 tsp sugar. Cook for a few minutes until just bubbling. Stir in drained spinach.

## WHITE SAUCE

6 Tbs (90ml) salted butter or margarine

6 Tbs (90ml) flour

4 cups (1 Litre) lowfat milk

2 cups (500ml) grated cheddar cheese

Salt and pepper

½ tsp (2.5ml) nutmeg

SAUCE: Melt butter or margarine in a medium pot. Stir in flour and allow to cook for 1 minute. Slowly add milk and whisk until thickened. Stir in cheddar cheese and taste for seasoning. Add salt, pepper and nutmeg as desired.

2 cups (500ml) grated mozzarella

Parmesan cheese for sprinkling (optional)

8 oz (250g) green lasagne noodles
  (no cooking required)

TO ASSEMBLE:
Spray an ovenproof dish. Place in alternate layers as described:

1 layer vegetables, 1 layer lasagne noodles,
1 layer white sauce, 1 layer noodles,
1 layer vegetables, 1 layer lasagne noodles,
1 layer white sauce.

The top layer of noodles must be well covered with the white sauce, or they will dry out.

Do not overlap the noodles as they will be too thick and will not cook through.

Top with cheese and parmesan (if desired).

Bake in a preheated 375 F (180 C) oven on middle rack for at least 60 to 75 mins or until lasagne feels soft when pricked in center.

TO FREEZE: Freeze unbaked. Defrost before baking. Bake as above.

SERVES: 15–20

# VEGETABLE SPRING ROLLS IN PHYLLO

These are just fabulous because they do not need to be fried. They make a great starter served with the sweet and sour sauce or as a vegetable accompaniment to any main course.

2 tsps (10ml) olive oil
1 carrot, julienned
4 baby zucchinis (marrows), julienned
2 celery sticks, cut into strips
6-oz can (1 x 230g tin) water chestnuts,
  sliced thinly
1 red pepper, cut into strips
3 scallions, cut on diagonal
¼ cabbage, finely shredded
8 oz (500g) bean sprouts
Seasoning salt
Herbamare
1 box phyllo (approx. 16 sheets)
Butter or margarine for brushing

Heat wok until very hot. Add oil.

Place cabbage and bean sprouts in wok and quickly stir-fry until liquid has evaporated. Remove and place in a colander.

Place all other vegetables in wok and stir-fry very quickly (seasoning very well at the same time) until just under-cooked.

Place both mixtures in a colander or strainer and allow excess liquid to drain. Mixture must be very dry or it will make phyllo soggy.

Brush each of 2 sheets of phyllo with either melted margarine or butter. Cut phyllo into 4 squares. Place a little mixture on each square and fold sides in first, then roll up.

Place on a baking sheet and brush outside with some margarine or butter.

Bake in a preheated 375 F (180 C) oven for 20 to 30 mins uncovered or until browned.

HANDY TIP: If freezing, defrost in fridge overnight and then bake as above.

NOTE: Before using phyllo bring it to room temperature or it cracks when cold.

## SWEET & SOUR SAUCE

¼ cup (60ml) vinegar
3 Tbs (45ml) sugar
2 tsps (10ml) salt
2 Tbs (30ml) tomato sauce (ketchup)
¾ cup (175ml) pineapple juice
2 tsps (10ml) cornstarch (maizena)
2 Tbs (30ml) oil

Heat all ingredients on a medium heat whisking until thickened. Allow to cool before serving. Sauce can be made and refrigerated a few days before serving.

SERVES: 8–10

Vegetable spring rolls in phyllo

Strawberry pavlova

ROASTED FRUIT SALAD

PAVLOVA WITH STRAWBERRY CREAM FILLING

# DESSERTS

EASY APPLE TART WITH CARAMEL SAUCE

MARS BAR ICE CREAM

Tropical fruit sundae

Of all the sections in this book, I am sure many of you will find desserts to be your favorite, as it is mine. I have tried to give you a nice variety from fruity to rich and decadent chocolate desserts. They are all contemporary recipes that suit our eating habits well. I've moved away from traditional, heavy desserts to the more fashionable and avant-garde.

The fruit desserts are spectacular because each one is different. When presented each will make a statement that is fresh and bold. Accompany any of them with other delectable desserts and your guest will be wowed.

Particularly in the ice cream recipes, which call for folded, beaten egg whites, it is terribly important not to over-fold the whites because you will lose the volume that is essential to the light texture of ice cream.

If you do not have a double boiler, create your own by placing a metal bowl over a pot of boiling water. It is the steam that is required for double-boiling, not the direct water. This method is more gentle than placing a pot directly on the stove.

# DESSERTS

BREAD & BUTTER PUDDING

CHOCOLATE PIZZA WITH ICE CREAM & STRAWBERRIES

COFFEE MERINGUE ICE CREAM

EASY APPLE TART WITH CARAMEL SAUCE

FRUITY GINGER TRIFLE

HOT CHOCOLATE PUDDINGS

LAYERED GINGER LOAF ICE CREAM

LAYERED CHOCOLATE ICE CREAM DELIGHT

MARS BAR ICE CREAM

NOUGAT ICE CREAM

PAVLOVA WITH STRAWBERRY CREAM FILLING

QUICK POACHED NECTARINES AND BERRIES

ROASTED FRUIT SALAD

TROPICAL FRUIT SUNDAE

## MARS BAR ICE CREAM

This ice cream is extra rich and extraordinarily delicious. Everyone will love it.

5 egg yolks
6 egg whites
3 3½-oz (3 x 100g) Mars Bars
1 cup (250ml) cream

**SAUCE:** 1 3½-oz (1 x 100g) Mars Bar and ⅓ cup cream, melted in microwave

Beat egg yolks in double boiler until thickened. Melt Mars Bars in microwave.

Add melted chocolate to egg yolks and continue to beat.

Beat egg whites until very stiff.
Beat cream until stiff.

Allow chocolate mixture to cool slightly. Add chocolate mixture to egg whites with the mixmaster running. Continue beating for a few minutes. Fold in beaten cream.

Melt cream and chocolate for sauce in microwave on high until runny.

Pour half of the ice cream in a plastic-wrap-lined 12-inch (30cm) loaf tin or in a glass bowl. Drizzle in some sauce. Then pour in remaining ice cream and lastly finish with more sauce.

Allow to set for a few hours or overnight.

Serve half-melted.

SERVES: 10–12

## BREAD & BUTTER PUDDING

You'll love this dessert because it's so easy to prepare and so delicious.

10 slices babke or cinnamon loaf
½ cup (125ml) flaked almonds, toasted

1½ cups (375ml) milk
¼ cup (60ml) finely granulated white sugar
1½ cups (375ml) cream
2 eggs
1 tsp (5ml) vanilla extract
½ cup (125ml) soft brown sugar

Slice babke. Place in a sprayed ovenproof dish, layering babke. Sprinkle with flaked almonds. (Add raisins if desired.)

Warm milk, cream and finely granulated white sugar and whisk in eggs and vanilla extract. Pour mixture over babke and leave for 15 mins to absorb.

Sprinkle with brown sugar and bake in preheated 375 F (180 C) oven for 45 mins or until golden.

SERVES: 8–10

Mars bar ice cream

Chocolate pizza with cream and strawberries

Layered chocolate ice cream delight

Layered ginger loaf ice cream

## CHOCOLATE PIZZA W/ICE CREAM & STRAWBERRIES

Whenever I make this dessert, everyone raves. It's so simple. The base can be made ahead. Top with balls of ice cream and decorate with strawberries just before serving.

### BASE

4½ oz (150g) dark chocolate

3 Tbs (100g) unsalted butter

1¼ cups (310ml) flour

½ tsp (2.5ml) baking powder

¼ tsp (1ml) salt

¾ cup (175ml) finely granulated white sugar

2 jumbo eggs

3½ oz (100g) pecan nuts, chopped

Preheat oven to 375 F (180 C). Line a 10-inch (26-cm) pizza plate or quiche dish with wax paper cut to fit dish and spray very well.

Melt butter and chocolate in double boiler or in microwave. Allow to cool slightly.

Cream sugar and eggs until light and fluffy. Add cooled chocolate mixture and beat for a few mins until thickened. Stir in flour, baking powder, salt and pecan nuts. Spread into prepared dish and bake for 20 mins on middle rack of oven.

Pizza should be firm, but slightly soft. Allow to cool. Peel off paper when cool.

SERVE WITH: Balls of vanilla ice cream, sliced strawberries, and drizzle with peppermint Aero sauce.

### CHOCOLATE PEPPERMINT SAUCE

3½ oz (100g) peppermint-flavored chocolate

½ to ¾ cup (125ml to 175ml) cream

Melt Aero and cream together and whisk until smooth.

SERVES: 8

HANDY TIP: Pizza base can be made 2 to 3 days ahead and kept covered. Sauce can also be made ahead and kept in fridge. Should sauce harden, soften in microwave for 30 to 40 seconds.

## COFFEE MERINGUE ICE CREAM

### MERINGUE

4 egg whites

1 cup (250ml) sugar

2 Tbs (30ml) strong coffee powder

Preheat oven to 250 F (120 C). Spray some baking paper and place on a baking sheet.

Beat egg whites and coffee powder until very stiff. Add sugar very slowly over 20 mins until egg whites look like marshmallows. Continue beating after adding sugar each time.

Spread on to a baking sheet and mold to look like a shell. Bake for 1 hour. Then turn oven off and leave to cool in oven. Do not allow to get too hard.

### ICE CREAM

4 eggs, separated

1 cup (250ml) cream or nondairy cream

¾ cup (175ml) finely granulated white sugar

2½ Tbs (37.5ml) strong coffee powder

2½ oz (80g) box vanilla instant pudding

Beat egg yolks, sugar and coffee until very thick.

Beat egg whites until very stiff.

Beat cream or nondairy cream until very thick. Stir in vanilla instant pudding to thicken at end.

Fold all three mixtures together.

TO ASSEMBLE: Shape meringue by bending it to fit into a 10-inch (26-cm) springform tin. Pour ice cream into center and allow to set. Remove springform tin when set and meringue will be completely free-standing. Keep frozen until ready to serve.

Toast some almonds to sprinkle on top before serving.

Allow ice cream to melt slightly before serving.

SERVES: 8–10

Coffee meringue ice cream

# EASY APPLE TART WITH CARAMEL SAUCE

The pastry is light and crunchy, and the filling tastes even better. Your guests will really enjoy this.

## CRUST

1½ cups (375ml) flour

4 Tbs (125g) unsalted butter

1 tsp (5ml) salt

½ cup (125ml) sugar

1 egg yolk

¼ cup (60ml) cream

8 Granny Smith apples,
  peeled, cored and sliced thinly

½ cup (125ml) sugar

2 Tbs (30ml) cinnamon

2 Tbs (30g) butter

1 egg yolk

¼ cup (125ml) milk

Place butter, flour, salt and sugar in food processor and process with metal blade to resemble crumbs. Combine yolk and cream and add to food processor. Pulse until dough just forms a ball. Do not overprocess.

Roll into a flat circle and place in a sprayed 10-inch (26-cm) loose-bottom tart tin or quiche dish. Mix sugar and cinnamon together.

Sprinkle with half cinnamon & sugar. Begin on one side and overlap apples in a pattern. Dot with butter and sprinkle with cinnamon and sugar again. Brush crust sides with egg & milk mixture.

Bake at 375 F (180 C) for 40 mins or until golden brown.

## CARAMEL SAUCE

¾ cup (175ml) sugar

⅓ cup (80ml) water

Lemon juice

½ cup (125ml) cream

1 Tbs (15ml) butter

In a small pot, combine sugar, water and lemon juice and cook on a medium heat until sugar starts to caramelize. WATCH CAREFULLY AND DO NOT TOUCH.

Lower heat and swirl around until it becomes golden. Heat cream gently and then stir in with butter. Continue stirring until smooth.

Drizzle over apple tart.

SERVES: 8

# FRUITY GINGER TRIFLE

My family loves ginger, so anything with ginger goes. Should you wish to substitute a vanilla sponge cake, you may do so. It is particularly nice with the bananas and looks very impressive when served in a beautiful glass bowl.

## GINGER CAKE

15 oz (450g) ginger cake

½ to ¾ cup (125 to 175ml) orange juice

4 egg yolks

¾ cup (175ml) finely granulated white sugar

1 cup (250ml) cream or nondairy cream

2 Tbs (30ml) lemon juice

Fruit—bananas, strawberries, mango

Beat egg yolks with sugar in a double boiler until very thick and stiff. Add lemon juice. Mixture must be very creamy.

Beat cream or nondairy cream until thick.

Cool egg yolk mixture and fold into cream. Set aside

Slice cake. Sprinkle cake slices with a little orange juice, just to moisten it. Make alternate layers starting with cake, custard, mango, cake, custard, banana, cake, custard, strawberries.

Can be made ahead. Keep refrigerated. Nondairy ginger cake can be used.

SERVES: 8–10

Easy apple tart with caramel sauce

Nougat ice cream

## HOT CHOCOLATE PUDDINGS

You might never recover from the rich chocolate taste of these wondrous puddings because they are something to remember.

6 egg yolks
6 eggs
10 oz (300g) dark Belgian chocolate
10 oz (300g) unsalted butter
⅓ cup (60g) flour

Preheat oven to 375 F (180 C). Line 10 small dariole (stainless steel) or glass ovenproof molds with butter and dust with sugar or brush the inside of a 10-inch (26-cm) ovenproof quiche dish with butter and dust with sugar.

Lightly beat eggs and yolks together just enough to mix them.

Melt chocolate and butter in microwave or in double boiler until melted. Cool slightly and then stir in to egg mixture.

Lastly fold in flour.

Fill molds ¾ full. Place in oven and bake for 10 to 12 minutes or until puddings are slightly puffed. Remove and unmold. Center must still be runny. Serve with ice cream.

SERVES: 10

## LAYERED GINGER LOAF ICE CREAM

The beauty of this ice cream is that it can be made and kept in the freezer. Should you not want to use ginger, you can substitute an ordinary syrup and vanilla cookies instead. It makes a wonderful nondairy ice cream.

8 cups (2 Litres) vanilla ice cream
  (dairy or nondairy)
1 packet ginger cookies, crushed

## GINGER BUTTERSCOTCH SAUCE

1 cup (250ml) sugar
½ cup (125ml) water
1 cup (250ml) cream or nondairy cream, warmed slightly
3 Tbs (45ml) butter or margarine
3 Tbs (45ml) chopped candied or crystallized ginger (or ginger in syrup, using 2 Tbs of syrup for extra flavor)

Boil sugar and water in a heavy pot on high heat until golden. Stir in cream or nondairy cream slowly with a wooden spoon, stirring all the time. Add butter or margarine and then stir in chopped ginger. Allow to cool.

### METHOD

Crush ginger cookies in food processor until very fine. Line a 12- to 14-inch (30- to 35-cm) loaf tin with plastic wrap, pressing plastic into sides and bottom of tin. Sprinkle some cookies on base of tin.

Melt ice cream slightly and spread some on top of cookies. Drizzle with some sauce.

Sprinkle another layer of cookies, another layer of ice cream and more sauce, ending with a thin layer of cookies.

Place one more layer of plastic wrap on top and press down to shape into tin.
Freeze until firm.

TO UNMOLD: Remove top layer of plastic and place a plate on top of tin. Invert tin, remove it and then remove plastic wrap.

SERVES: 10–12

HANDY TIP: Allow ice cream to soften for at least 15 to 20 mins before serving (if using dairy ice cream). Do not remove from tin until softened.

Nondairy ice cream will never set absolutely firmly, therefore no need to remove from freezer too early.

Hot chocolate puddings

# LAYERED CHOCOLATE
# ICE CREAM DELIGHT

The contrast between the cake layers, the sauce and the ice cream will tantalize all tastebuds. You won't be sorry to have made this dessert.

## ICE CREAM

If you are not making this nondairy, then you can purchase ready-made (16-cup or 2-litre) vanilla ice cream.

4 eggs, separated
1 cup (250ml) nondairy cream
½ cup (125ml) finely granulated white sugar
1 tsp (5ml) vanilla extract

Beat egg yolks and sugar until very thick, pale and creamy. Add vanilla extract.

Beat egg whites until stiff. Beat nondairy cream until stiff.

Fold all three mixtures together and place in freezer to set.

## CHOCOLATE SAUCE

1 lb (500g) dark chocolate
4 Tbs (60ml) margarine or butter
3 Tbs (45ml) caramel or corn syrup
¾ cup (175ml) cream or nondairy cream

Melt chocolate with syrup in a pot over a low heat. Add margarine or butter when melted and then stir in nondairy cream. Bring to a boil and allow to boil on a medium-low heat until slightly thickened or for approx. 8 mins.

Allow to cool.

14½ oz (450g) un-iced chocolate cake
  (nondairy chocolate cake may also be used)

TO ASSEMBLE: Place a thin layer of cake on bottom of a deep glass dish. Spread with some ice cream. Drizzle with some chocolate sauce. Add another layer of cake, more ice cream and more sauce. Continue until you have reached top of dish or finished your mixtures.

NOTE: Chocolate sauce may be frozen and reheated in microwave. If sauce thickens too much to spread, place in microwave for 30 to 40 seconds on high.

SERVES: 12–15

# NOUGAT ICE CREAM

Whenever I make this ice cream, not only is it delectable, but it looks great. I like to make ice creams in a loaf tin because they cut easily, and are easy to serve.

5 jumbo eggs, separated
¾ cup (375ml) sugar
½ cup (125ml) cream cheese
7 oz (200g) caramel roasted nuts
  (almonds and pecans)
1 cup (250ml) cream
Red cherries (optional)

Whisk egg yolks and sugar in a double boiler until thickened.

Beat egg whites in mixmaster. Add hot egg yolks to stiff whites, and with the machine running, continue beating until glossy and yolks have cooled down.

Beat cream until stiff. Gently fold in cream cheese. Take a little egg white mixture and stir into cream mixture to lighten the weight of it. Then fold all mixtures gently together until mixed through. Stir in nuts and cherries.

Set in a 12- to 14-inch (30- to 35-cm) loaf tin or a glass bowl.

HANDY TIP: There is no need to line or spray tin before filling with ice cream. Remove ice cream from tin as soon as it is set and keep in tinfoil until ready to use.

Soften ice cream before serving.

SERVES: 10–12

Quick poached nectarines and berries

Roasted fruit salad

## PAVLOVA WITH STRAWBERRY CREAM FILLING

This pavlova looks wonderful with its pretty pink filling. It makes a nice change from ordinary cream and is just the kind of dessert that everyone loves.

4 egg whites
1 tsp (5ml) cream of tartar
1 cup (250ml) sugar

Preheat oven to 250 F (120 C). Spray wax paper with nonstick cooking spray and place on a baking tray.

Beat egg whites until frothy. Then add cream of tartar. Beat until stiff and then slowly add sugar over 20 mins until meringue is very thick and resembles marshmallows.

Spread on to wax paper in circle shape approx. 10 inch (26cm) and build up sides with a small knife. Bake for 50 to 60 mins and then turn oven off and leave in oven for 1 hour to cool.

### FILLING
4 egg yolks
¾ cup (175ml) sugar
16 oz (500g) strawberries, puréed with
  ⅓ cup confectioner's sugar
1 cup (250ml) cream or nondairy cream
1 Tbs (15ml) gelatin, softened and dissolved

Beat egg yolks and sugar in a double boiler over low heat continuously for 20 mins until mixture thickens and is very stiff. Allow to cool in fridge for at least 15 mins.

Purée strawberries with confectioner's sugar until smooth. Dissolve gelatine in 1 Tbs (15ml) cold water and then 1 Tbs (15ml) warm water. Stir into strawberry mixture. Mix strawberries and egg yolk mixture together.

Beat cream or nondairy cream until stiff. Fold strawberry mixture into whipped cream. Allow to set.

Fill meringue with strawberry cream filling 1 hour before serving to allow meringue to soften. Decorate with piles of fresh strawberries.

HANDY TIP: Place empty pavlova shell on serving platter before filling, or you will not be able to lift it.

Pavlova can be made and kept for up to 2 weeks ahead (unfilled). Keep well covered and in a dry place.

SERVES: 10–12

## QUICK POACHED NECTARINES AND BERRIES

I have made this dessert at least 1,000 times, because it is so easy and so wonderful. It is also fat free, so everyone loves it.

10-12 nectarines or peaches
  (or canned peaches when out of season)
8 oz (250g) blueberries
8 oz (250g) raspberries
8 oz (250g) strawberries
¾ cup (175ml) sugar
3 Tbs (45ml) orange-flavored liqueur

Cut nectarines or peaches into quarters with the skin on, but with pit removed. Pour sugar over them and place them in a medium pot and allow to heat through on medium high heat. Simmer for 5 mins.

Remove from heat and allow to cool slightly. Toss in berries and sprinkle with liqueur. Place in fridge until ready to serve.

SERVE WITH:
1½ cups (2 x 175ml) fruit yogurt
1 cup (250ml) thick cream

Stir yogurt and thick cream together and place in an attractive serving bowl. Top very generously with soft brown sugar only about 1 hour before serving.

This must be made the day you wish to serve it as the fresh fruit loses its color. The berries help to hide the marks that fresh fruit picks up.

SERVES: 8–10

## ROASTED FRUIT SALAD

It is so nice to have a different fruit salad. This one is particularly delicious and will also be nice should you have to serve any diabetics.

4 pears, unpeeled, cut into quarters

4 apples, unpeeled, cut into quarters

4 bananas, cut into big chunks

2 pineapples, sliced and cut into quarters

16 oz (500g) strawberries, whole

1 packet dried apricots

4 oranges, cut into segments

1 cup (250ml) fresh orange juice

Grated rind of 1 orange

3 to 4 tsps (15 to 30ml) sugar

¾ cup (175ml) apricot jam
  (or diabetic apricot jam)

Switch on broiler in oven. Element should be red.

Place all cut up fruit except bananas and strawberries in a roasting pan, with ½ cup orange juice, orange rind and sugar.

Grill fruit on bottom rack of oven for 20 mins. Shake pan gently and add bananas and strawberries.

Add more orange juice only if necessary, as fruit will make its own juice. Place roasting pan back in oven for a further 15 mins.

Just before serving stir in jam and place back under the grill to heat through. Be careful, as fruit will burn because of jam. Do not place too close to broiler.Serve warm or at room temperature with ice cream or custard.

SERVES: 8–10

## TROPICAL FRUIT SUNDAE

Of all the desserts that I make, this one is very special. It is layered, colorful and sensational with the mango puree between the layers of fruit.

6 to 8 cups (1+ ½ Litres) fresh mangoes,
  puréed (in season). Bulk with puréed
  papinoes if necessary (you need to have
  6 to 8 cups of purée when finished)

Honeydew melon, chunks

Cataloupe (spanspek), chunks

Pineapple, chunks

Canned (tinned) or fresh litchis

Bananas, sliced

In a deep glass trifle dish, layer fruits in varying colors, spreading a thin layer of mango puree between each section of fruit.

Begin with honeydew melon, then pineapple, cantaloupe (spanspek), litchis and lastly bananas, making sure that bananas are well covered with mango purée to prevent discoloration.

Decorate with whole fresh strawberries.

SERVES: 10–12

Phyllo crisps

LEMON MASCARPONE CAKE

UPSIDE DOWN APPLE CAKE

# BAKING

GINGER-DATE MUFFINS

MACADAMIA & CHOCOLATE WAFERS

I love baking as long as it is not too complicated and involved.

For me baking is all about little bits and pieces and being able to nibble on delicious tidbits.

There is nothing nicer than freshly baked cookies or muffins, and because they don't require a lot of preparation, they should be made the day you serve them.

Always preheat your oven, so that it is ready for you when you have finished making your mixture. I always bake in the middle of the oven, unless you have a thermofan oven, in which case you can bake on any rack.

As you can see from the recipes I love mascarpone because it has a subtlety and creaminess without the sourness of cream cheese.

You will notice that I have specified "jumbo" eggs. These are the only ones I use in all my recipes.

# BAKING

WHITE CHOCOLATE CHIP BROWNIES

PHYLLO CRISPS

UPSIDE DOWN APPLE CAKE

LEMON MASCARPONE CAKE

MACADAMIA & CHOCOLATE WAFERS

APPLE CINNAMON MUFFINS

GINGER-DATE MUFFINS

AMARETTO MASCARPONE CHEESECAKE

ALMOND BISCOTTI

WARM CHOCOLATE PECAN CAKE WITH VANILLA MASCARPONE SAUCE

## ALMOND BISCOTTI

If you are looking for a low-fat cookie, then this is for you. Crisp and crunchy, these biscotti are sliced very thinly and make a large quantity. If you don't want nuts, substitute chocolate chips.

4 egg whites

¾ cup (175ml) finely granulated white sugar

1 cup (250ml) flour

7 oz (200g) blanched almonds, toasted

Preheat oven to 350 F (160 C).

Line a small loaf tin with baking paper on the bottom, and spray sides and bottom.

In a mixmaster, beat egg whites until stiff. Add sugar. Then fold in nuts and flour.

Spread into loaf tin. Bake for 30 to 35 mins or until lightly golden. Turn oven off and leave in oven for 20 mins to cool.

Remove from tin when cooled. Allow to cool completely and then slice into very thin slices. Place back in 250 F (120 C) oven to toast until lightly golden and dried out.

Keeps very well in Tupperware.

SERVES: 8–10

## AMARETTO MASCARPONE CHEESECAKE

With all the added calories, don't miss a slice of this velvety cake. It is best served at room temperature so that the cheese does not set and is not cold. If making a day ahead of time, place back in a very low oven to warm through.

### BASE

3½ oz (100g) amaretto cookies

3½ oz (100g) tennis cookies or other coconut cookies

4 Tbs (60ml) butter, melted

¼ cup (60ml) sugar

Crush cookies in food processor. Add melted butter and sugar until just mixed. Spread on bottom and halfway up sides of 10-inch (26-cm) ungreased springform tin. Bake on 375 F (180 C) for 15 mins until set. Remove from oven and allow to cool.

### FILLING

2 cups (2 x 250ml) mascarpone cheese

1 cup (250ml) creamed smooth cottage cheese or cream cheese

1 cup (250ml) sour cream

3 jumbo eggs, separated

⅔ cup (175ml) finely granulated white sugar (divided into ⅓ cup and ⅓ cup)

3 Tbs (45ml) flour

1 tsp (5ml) vanilla extract

4.5 oz (150g) caramelized pecans or almonds, chopped (see substitutes)

Preheat oven to 350 F (160 C).

In a mixmaster, beat 3 egg yolks with ⅓ cup sugar until very creamy. Add mascarpone and continue to beat until thickened. Add cream cheese, flour, sour cream and vanilla and beat on low just to mix through.

Beat egg whites with remaining ⅓ cup sugar and continue to beat until very stiff. Fold some whites into mascarpone mixture. Then fold in remaining whites. Pour ½ into tin. Sprinkle with some caramelized nuts and top with remaining mixture.

Bake for 1 hour on middle rack. Turn oven off and leave in oven for 1 hour to cool.

### TOPPING

1 cup (250ml) mascarpone cheese

1 cup (250ml) sour cream

⅓ cup (80ml) finely granulated white sugar

1¾ oz (50g) caramelized pecans

When cake has cooled for at least 2 to 3 hours, spread with topping and allow it to seep in. Sprinkle with remaining chopped nuts.

SERVES: 6–8

Amaretto mascarpone cheesecake

## APPLE CINNAMON MUFFINS

I love the combination of apple and cinnamon, so these muffins are full of both. Be careful not to eat them all before you serve them.

6 Tbs (90g) unsalted butter
1 cup (250ml) milk
2 jumbo eggs
2 heaped cups (500ml) self-raising flour
½ cup (125ml) finely granulated white sugar
1 tsp (5ml) baking powder

2 or 3 red apples, peeled and chopped
¾ cup (175ml) sugar
1½ heaped Tbs (22ml) cinnamon

Preheat oven to 375 F (180 C).

Melt butter. Add milk and beaten eggs to butter and set aside.

Mix together the flour, sugar and baking powder.

Stir the wet ingredients into the dry and do not mix too well. Mixture should be a little lumpy. Stir in chopped apples, keeping a few for the top.

Mix together the ¾ cup sugar and the cinnamon.

Spray and flour 12 muffin tins. Half fill tins, then sprinkle with a lot of cinnamon-sugar. Then fill again and top with more cinnamon-sugar. Top with some apples.

Bake for 25 mins or until golden.

MAKES 12 MUFFINS

## GINGER-DATE MUFFINS

If you love ginger, these will really grab you—and they only take a minute to make. The dates make them really soft and moist.

1¼ cups (310ml) cake flour
1 tsp (5ml) baking powder
¼ tsp (1.5ml) bicarbonate of soda
6 Tbs (90ml) soft brown sugar
6 Tbs (90ml) unsalted butter
1 jumbo egg
1 cup (250g) pitted dates
¾ cup (175ml) buttermilk or plain yogurt
3 Tbs (45ml) ginger pieces and syrup

Preheat oven to 380 F (190 C).

Spray and flour 12 muffin tins. Set aside.

In a food processor, process the butter and sugar until smooth. Add egg and continue to process. Then add dates (It is best to soften dates in microwave for 30 to 40 secs) and ginger in syrup. Process until smooth. Remove from food processor.

Stir in buttermilk and finally all dry ingredients (flour, baking powder and bicarbonate). Do not over mix.

Spoon into muffin tins until three-quarters full and sprinkle with some Jungle Oats or Instant Oats.

Bake for 20 mins or a little longer until tester comes out clean. Allow to cool.

MAKES 10 MUFFINS

Apple cinnamon muffins

## LEMON MASCARPONE CAKE

This is a delicious, light cake that is great at tea time.

5 egg whites

2 tsps (10ml) baking powder

5 egg yolks

1 tsp (5ml) vanilla extract

½ cup (125ml) oil

½ cup (125ml) boiling water

½ cup (125ml) finely granulated white sugar

¼ cup (60ml) lemon juice

1 heaped cup (250ml + 30ml) flour

1½ tsps (7.5ml) baking powder

Rind of 1 lemon

Preheat oven to 375 F (180 C). Spray and flour 2 9-inch (24 cm) springform or layer tins.

Beat egg yolks with vanilla. Add oil, boiling water and lemon juice and continue beating all the time until foamy. Add sugar and continue beating.

Lastly add flour, baking powder and lemon rind.

Beat egg whites with baking powder until very stiff. Set aside.

Fold egg whites into lemon mixture.

Bake for 20 to 25 mins on middle rack of oven. Allow to cool.

### MASCARPONE

1 cup (250ml) mascarpone cheese

2 eggs, separated

⅓ cup (80ml) finely granulated white sugar

3 Tbs (45ml) lemon juice

1 tsp (5ml) lemon rind

Beat egg yolks with sugar until very thick. Add lemon juice. Add mascarpone and continue beating until thickened.

Beat egg whites until stiff. Fold into egg yolk and add lemon rind. Place mixture in fridge and allow to set.

Spread half the mascarpone on top of bottom layer of cake. Top with other cake and more mascarpone. Decorate with grated lemon rind.

SERVES: 8–10

## MACADAMIA & CHOCOLATE WAFERS

These can be made ahead; they keep very well in an airtight container, but don't keep opening the container, or there won't be any to serve your guests. Too delicious for words.

10 Tbs (200g) unsalted butter, softened

1½ cups (375ml) finely granulated
   white sugar

½ cup (125ml) carmel syrup or
   ordinary syrup

1 heaped cup (250ml + 30ml) flour

4 egg whites

6½ oz (200g) macadamia nut pieces

¾ cup (175ml) chocolate chips

Preheat oven to 350 F (160 C).

In a food processor, blend the butter, sugar, syrup, flour and egg whites until completely smooth.

Spread the mixture very thinly on to sprayed baking paper on 2 large baking sheets. Sprinkle with nuts and chocolate chips.

Bake in oven until quite dark and golden (15 to 20 mins). Watch them and don't allow them to burn. Cool. Break into pieces and keep in airtight container until ready to use.

SERVES: 8–10

Macadamia & chocolate wafers

## PHYLLO CRISPS

When you want your guests to think you're a genius, serve these with a nice dessert or with coffee. Once you start, you can't stop eating them.

3 sheets phyllo
½ cup (125ml) pecans
½ cup (125ml) sugar
4 Tbs (90ml) butter or margarine
  for brushing

Preheat oven to 350 F (160 C).
Process pecans and sugar in food processor until finely ground. Set aside.

Place baking paper on a large baking sheet.

Brush 1 sheet of phyllo with butter or margarine. Place brushed phyllo on baking paper. Sprinkle half the nut-sugar mixture on first phyllo sheet.

Top phyllo with another sheet. Brush and sprinkle with remaining nut-sugar mixture. Top with last sheet of phyllo. Brush with butter or margarine and press down with your hand.

Chill for 20 mins. Remove from fridge and cut into long triangles. You should get about 48 to 64 triangles per 3 sheets.

Top with more baking paper and bake in lower part of oven for 15 mins or until golden. Cool on baking sheet.

NOTE: Watch them carefully to ensure they don't burn.

SERVES: 6–8

## UPSIDE DOWN APPLE CAKE

This is one of the quickest and easiest cakes you'll make, and it turns out delicious each time. Serve warmed. If you have inverted it, place in the microwave and reheat for 3 to 4 mins. Serve with vanilla ice cream or custard if you wish to serve it for dessert.

6 apples, peeled and sliced thinly
¼ cup (60g) butter or margarine
⅔ cup (160ml) soft brown sugar
  (dark brown sugar)

Preheat oven to 350 F (160 C).

Melt butter or margarine and brown sugar in a frying pan. Add apples. Lower heat to medium high and sauté apples until just softened. Set aside.

1⅓ cups (320ml) flour
2 Tbs (30ml) self-raising flour
1 tsp (5ml) baking powder
Pinch of salt
1 cup (250ml) soft brown sugar
6 Tbs (90g) butter or margarine
2 eggs
½ cup (125ml) milk or orange juice
1 tsp (5ml) vanilla extract

In a mixmaster bowl, beat butter or margarine and sugar until very creamy. Add eggs and continue beating.

Add flour, self-raising flour, baking powder and salt. Mix together gently. Pour in milk or orange juice and vanilla extract.

Beat well until nice and creamy.

Spray and flour a 10-inch (26-cm) baking tin or other deep baking tin of the same size. Place apples and the sauce in the bottom of the tin. Then pour batter over the apples.

Place on the middle rack of the oven and bake for 30 to 40 mins or until a toothpick comes out clean.

Run a knife around the edge and turn the cake upside down onto a serving plate.

SERVES: 8–10

Upside down apple cake

Almond biscotti

## WARM CHOCOLATE PECAN CAKE WITH VANILLA MASCARPONE SAUCE

Rich and moist in texture, this cake makes an ideal dessert or tea item. It will take less than 20 minutes to make.

4 eggs
⅔ cup (160ml) finely granulated white sugar
3½ oz (100g) dark cooking chocolate
4 Tbs (60g) butter
⅔ cup (160ml) self-raising flour
1 cup (250ml) chopped pecans
1 tsp (5ml) vanilla extract

Preheat oven to 350 F (160 C). Spray and flour a loose-bottom tart tin or a 10-inch (26-cm) springform tin.

Beat eggs in mixmaster until very thick and light yellow. Then add sugar and continue beating.

Meanwhile melt chocolate and butter in microwave. Stir until mixture is smooth.

Add chocolate mixture to eggs and continue beating until slightly thickened. Then gently fold in flour, vanilla extract and pecans.

Place in presprayed tin and bake for 20 mins. Turn oven off and allow to remain in oven for another 10 mins. Keep cake in tin and then warm it in a low oven for 15 to 20 mins just before serving.

### MASCARPONE SAUCE

¼ cup (60ml) finely granulated white sugar
8 oz (1 X 250g) mascarpone cheese
2 tsps (10ml) vanilla extract
½ cup (125ml) milk

Stir all ingredients together. Sauce can be refrigerated until ready to serve.

TO SERVE: Cut slices of cake and then spoon a little sauce over the top of slice.

SERVES: 8–10

## WHITE CHOCOLATE CHIP BROWNIES

One of my all-time favorites to serve with coffee after a meal. They always satisfy the chocolate craving, but be careful 'cause they're quite rich.

12 Tbs (180ml) unsalted butter, melted
12 oz (375g) dark cooking chocolate

4 jumbo eggs
½ tsp (2.5ml) salt
1⅓ cups (340ml) sugar
2 tsps (10ml) vanilla extract
½ cup (125ml) flour
8 oz (250g) white chocolate,
  broken into pieces
2 cups (500ml) pecan pieces

Preheat oven to 350 F (160 C).

Line a small roasting pan with baking paper. Spray with nonstick cooking spray and dust lightly with flour. Melt butter and chocolate in microwave until smooth. Allow to cool slightly.

In a mixmaster, beat eggs very well on high until thick and light. Add salt and gradually add sugar while beating continuously. Beat in vanilla. Fold in chocolate mixture. Then fold in flour, white chocolate and pecans.

Pour batter into prepared pan. Bake for 50 mins or until tester comes out clean. Cool well before cutting. Leave in tin until cool. Can be kept in a tupperware for a few days or frozen. Dust with icing sugar before serving.

HANDY TIP: Dot your pan with some margarine to secure paper before spreading it with mixture. If the brownies rise quite a lot and then drop, press down gently with the palm of your hand before removing from the tin.

SERVES: 8–10

Warm Chocolate pecan cake with vanilla mascarpone sauce

Potato gnocchi topped with mixed vegetables

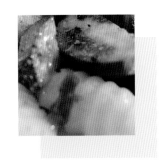

BAKED POTATO ROSTI

JASMINE RICE

# PULSES & GRAINS

LAYERED POTATO BAKE

RICE PILAF

I think that accompaniments to main courses are essential. They round off the meal and provide that little extra to your main course.

The potato dishes I have given you in this section are wonderful because they are not deep fried in tons of oil, yet they are as delicious.

Rice has also become more flexible; it is no longer just boiled or steamed, but rather lends itself to a variety of tasty additions.

# PULSES AND GRAINS

BAKED POTATO ROSTI

LAYERED POTATO BAKE

FRIED SWEET POTATO SLICES

JASMINE RICE

POTATO GNOCCHI TOPPED WITH MIXED VEGETABLES

RICE PILAF

ROASTED BUTTERNUT &  MUSHROOM RISOTTO

## BAKED POTATO ROSTI

This is such a simple dish but a great accompaniment to the main course. The quantity decreases as the potatoes cook, so make an extra amount because your guests will come back for more and more.

4 potatoes, unpeeled
Olive oil
Salt and pepper

Preheat oven to 450 F (220 C).

Slice potatoes with a mandoline. Line baking sheet with baking paper; spray paper with olive oil. Place potato slices on paper. Drizzle potatoes with olive oil and season with salt and pepper. Bake for 15 to 20 mins uncovered. Toss gently and turn oven down to 375 F (180 C). Continue baking until completely golden. Do not overbrown them.

SERVES: 3–4

## LAYERED POTATO BAKE

When you need a change from the usual potatoes, this is an outstanding potato dish because it can be prebaked. It's a good all-time favorite.

6 potatoes
2 cups (500ml) chicken stock
  (1 Knorr or 2 Telma cubes)
3 Tbs (45ml) butter or margarine
Salt and pepper to taste

Preheat oven to 375 F (180 C).

Spray an ovenproof baking dish with nonstick cooking spray.

Cut potatoes very thinly lengthwise with or without the skin on. Place in overlapping layers in rows in a baking dish. Dot with margarine or butter and season with salt and pepper.

Gently pour in half the stock. Place uncovered on the middle rack of the oven and bake for at least 45 mins or until liquid has evaporated.

Then pour in remaining stock and continue cooking until potatoes are soft and liquid has evaporated, approximately another 30 to 40 minutes.

This dish can be baked before serving and reheated as long as the potatoes are cooked through. Do not overbake if reheating.

OPTIONAL: ½ cup cream may be poured over the potatoes just before the end of the cooking period.

SERVES: 4–6

## FRIED SWEET POTATO SLICES

Slice sweet potatoes or yams with skin lengthways very thinly with skin on and fry in hot oil until browned and crisp.

## JASMINE RICE

Wash rice until water runs clear. Mix equal quantities of water to dry rice, i.e. 1 cup (250ml) rice to 1 cup (250ml) water. Bring to a boil in a large pot. Turn stove to low and simmer with lid on for 20 mins. Take off stove and allow rice to steam with the lid on for 10 mins. Serve immediately or allow to cool.

## POTATO GNOCCHI TOPPED WITH MIXED VEGETABLES

It is a pleasure to buy ready-made potato gnocchi and simply pop them into some boiling water. Top with this delicious sauce and you have a wonderful addition to any fish, meat or poultry dishe. Substitute orrechiette (ear-shaped) pasta if gnocchi are not available.

2 lbs (1kg) ready-made potato gnocchi or
  orecchiette (pasta)

Bring a large pot of water to a boil. Add 2 tsps salt to the water. Cook gnocchi in rapidly boiling water for approximately 5 minutes or until cooked through as per directions on packet. Drain and toss with olive oil.

## SAUCE

⅓ cup (80ml) olive oil

7 oz (200g) Italian red cherry tomatoes,
  cut in half

4 scallions, cut into thin slices

7 oz (200g) baby zucchinis (marrows),
  sliced thinly

1 small eggplant, skin on, cut into cubes
  (or 8 baby eggplant, cut lengthwise into
  quarters, skin on)

8 oz (250g) button mushrooms, cut in half

3 Tbs (45ml) fresh basil, chopped

½ cup (125ml) sun-dried tomatoes,
  chopped finely

2 tsps (10ml) sugar

1 cup (250ml) precooked tomato sauce

Salt

Freshly ground black pepper

Heat olive oil gently in a large frying pan. Sauté baby zucchinis, eggplant and mushrooms in pan seasoning generously with salt and pepper. Cook on medium heat until they are softened ± 5 minutes. Place cherry tomatoes and scallions in the pan and sauté until slightly soft.

Stir in basil, sun-dried tomatoes, tomato sauce and sugar and mix well. Taste for seasoning and add salt and pepper if necessary. Allow to cook for a few more minutes.

TO SERVE: Place gnocchi on a serving platter. Top with vegetables.

NOTE: The sauce can be made up to 3 days before and reheated. Undercook vegetables slightly if you make the sauce in advance.

SERVES: 6–8

# RICE PILAF

*A quick, colorful rice with a light crunch.*

1½ cups (375ml) long grain rice

¼ cup (60ml) finely chopped scallion

3 Tbs (45ml) butter or margarine

1 red pepper, chopped

1 yellow pepper, chopped

¼ cup (60ml) chopped parsley

¼ cup (60ml) finely chopped carrots

¼ cup (60ml) sesame seeds

Toast sesame seeds on a baking sheet in 300 F (140 C) oven for 10 mins until golden.

## SAUCE

2½ cups (625ml) chicken stock
  (1½ Knorr or 2 Telma cubes)

2 Tbs (30ml) light soya sauce

½ tsp (2.5ml) salt

½ tsp (2.5ml) nutmeg

Wash rice well until water is clear.

Melt butter or margarine on medium heat in a large pot. Add scallions and sauté until softened. Add rice and cook until coated with margarine or butter. Add chicken stock, soy sauce, salt and nutmeg. Stir and bring to a boil.

Cover and reduce heat to very low. Simmer for 20 mins. Then add chopped peppers, parsley and carrots. Leave for 5 to 10 mins off the stove with the lid on. Lastly add sesame seeds.

Taste for seasoning.

SERVES: 8–10

## ROASTED BUTTERNUT & MUSHROOM RISOTTO

*The roasted butternut gives a sweet, nutty taste to this risotto. Be careful not to overcook the rice or it becomes porridge.*

2 cups (500ml) arborio**
1 onion, finely chopped (red if available)
3 Tbs (45ml) olive oil
½ cup (125ml) white wine
4 cups (1 Litre) vegetable stock
  (8 tsps Maggi powder or 10 Telma)*
7 oz (100g) shitake mushrooms,
  sliced thinly (if available)
  or 3½ oz (50g) dry porcini mushrooms

1 whole butternut [¾ lb (450g)],
  cut into small chunks
2 Tbs (30ml) olive oil
Salt and pepper
Herbamare, freshly ground herbs

1 scallion, very finely sliced
Chopped parsley

Preheat oven to 450 F (220 C). Place butternut in a roasting pan, sprinkle with olive oil and seasonings. Bake for 20 to 25 mins or until quite brown on all sides.

Sauté onion in olive oil until just softened. Then add raw uncooked rice and sauté on medium high heat until rice turns golden. Add extra olive oil if necessary. Add white wine and simmer for a few minutes or until absorbed.

Slowly add vegetable stock a little at a time, turning heat down to low. Add mushrooms halfway through cooking. Stir rice each time you add stock, allowing rice to absorb the stock. Cooking should take 20 mins at least. Rice should taste a little crunchy.

Toss in scallion and butternut just before serving.

SERVES: 4–6

* If dry porcini mushrooms are available, soak 3½ oz (50g) dry porcini in 1½ cups boiling water for about 20 minutes. When soft, drain liquid and use same 1½ cups liquid and 2½ cups vegetable stock (5 tsps Maggi powder or 6 Telma) to make up the 4 cups stock listed in ingredients

** Italian rice for cooking risotto.

Roasted butternut & mushroom risotto

# SUGGESTED MENU IDEAS

# CONVERSIONS &

# SUBSTITUTES

# SUGGESTED MENU IDEAS

## LIGHT LUNCH FOR 4–6 PEOPLE

## LOW FAT DINNER

## LOW FAT LUNCH

## NONDAIRY DINNER

## CHOLESTEROL FREE DINNER

## FANCY DINNER FOR 4–6 PEOPLE

## FRIDAY NIGHT FAMILY DINNER

# SUBSTITUTES & CONVERSIONS

## OVEN TEMPERATURES

| C | 100 | 120 | 140 | 160 | 180 | 200 | 220 | 240 | 260 | 280 |
|---|-----|-----|-----|-----|-----|-----|-----|-----|-----|-----|
| F | 200 | 250 | 300 | 350 | 375 | 400 | 425 | 450 | 475 | 500 |

## MEASUREMENTS USED IN THIS BOOK

| METRIC | U.S. EQUIVALENTS |
|--------|------------------|
| 2.5ml | ½ tsp |
| 5ml | 1 tsp |
| 7.5ml | 1½ tsp |
| 10ml | 2 tsps |
| 15ml | 1 Tbs |

## LIQUID CAPACITY

| METRIC | U.S. EQUIVALENTS |
|--------|------------------|
| 60ml | ¼ cup |
| 80ml | ⅓ cup |
| 125ml | ½ cup |
| 160ml | ⅔ cup |
| 175ml | ¾ cup |
| 250ml | 1 cup |
| 375ml | 1½ cup |
| 500ml | 2 cups |
| 750ml | 3 cups |
| 1 litre | 4 cups |
| 1.5litres | 6 cups |
| 2 litres | 8 cups |

## WEIGHTS

| | |
|--------|------------------|
| 30g | 1 oz |
| 60g | 2 oz |
| 90g | 3 oz |
| 125g | 4 oz |
| 155g | 5 oz |
| 180g | 6 oz |
| 220g | 7 oz |
| 250g | 8 oz |
| 310g | 10 oz |
| 375g | 12 oz |
| 500g | 1 lb or 16 oz |
| 750g | 1½ lbs |
| 1 kg | 2 lbs |

# SUBSTITUTES & CONVERSIONS

## TIN MEASUREMENTS

| | | | |
|---|---|---|---|
| Smallest biscuit tray (baking sheet) | | 13½ x 9½ x ⅛ inch | 34 x 24 x 0.6 cm |
| Large biscuit tray (baking sheet) | | 17 x 11 x 1 inch | 44 x 49 x 2.5 cm |
| Small biscuit tray (baking sheet) | | 14½ x 10 x ¼ inch | 37 x 25 x 1 cm |
| Loaf tins | –small | 8 x 3½ x 2¾ inches | 20 x 8.5 x 7 cm |
| | –medium | 10 x 3½ x 2¾ inches | 26 x 8.5 x 7 cm |
| | –large | 14 x 4 x 3 inches | 35 x 11 x 7.5 cm |
| Pizza baking tin | | 12 inches | 31 cm diameter |
| Springform tins | | 9 inches | 24 cm |
| | | 10 inches | 26 cm |
| Tart tins | –small | 10 inches | 26 cm diameter |
| | –large | 11 inches | 28 cm diameter |
| Quiche | –large | 11 inches | 28 cm |
| Roasting pan | –small | 11 x 9 x 2 inches | 29 x 22 x 5 cm |
| Roasting pan | –large | 13 x 16 x 4½ inches | 34 x 24 x 5 cm |

## ALTITUDE CHANGES

The recipes in this book were tested at high altitude. This guide will help you alter your recipes accordingly if you are baking at sea level.

Baking powder—Increase by ¼ tsp (0 to 0.5ml) for each 1 tsp (5ml) required.

Sugar—Increase by 1 to 2 tsp (5-10ml) for each 1 cup (250ml) required.

Liquid—Decrease 1 to 2 Tbs (15-30ml) liquid per 1 cup (250ml) required.

Flour—Decrease by 1 Tbs (15ml) per 1 cup (250ml) required.

Baking temperature—Lower temperature by 25 F (10 C) and bake slightly longer.

## SALT AND PEPPER

In all my recipes I use freshly ground coarse sea salt. I am a generous salt user (for those who know me), and I like the flavor of the natural salt.

I also use freshly ground black pepper instead of any bottled pepper. You get a more natural taste from fresh black pepper.

# SUBSTITUTES FOR PRODUCTS USED IN RECIPES

CHINESE FOOD—I have found that many supermarkets carry various brands of these products, but any Chinese store will have all the ingredients.

*Tah Tsai/Chinese Cabbage*—If available, a wonderful alternative to ordinary spinach, which is not bitter.

*Bak Choy/Chinese Spinach*—If available, this does not contain as much water as normal cabbage; has more color and flavor.

*Marin/Japanese Sweet Wine*—eg: 1 tsp sugar + 1 Tbs syrup + ¾ cup water boiled for a few minutes to dissolve sugar. Bottle this amount and then take your measurements from this quantity. Mixture will keep in a bottle in your pantry.

*Rice Vinegar*—Substitute with apple cider vinegar diluted with water, e.g., ½ cup apple cider vinegar diluted with 4 Tbs water. This can be mixed and stored in a bottle.

*Soy Sauce*—I use Kikkoman.

*Palm Sugar*—This is a solid sugar from Thailand, which dissolves when mixed with liquids. It is readily available at any store that sells Chinese products.

*Sweet Chili Sauce*—A sweet, but spicy sauce to enhance many Thai-flavored dishes. Substitute by using chilli powder mixed with apricot jam, e.g., 1 Tbs = ½ tsp chili powder + 1 Tbs apricot jam.

*Yellow Miso Paste*—Japanese paste used in miso soup. Quite salty in flavor. Red Miso paste is also available.

*Coconut Milk*—I always use coconut milk instead of coconut cream. I find that they are almost identical and the milk is not as thick.

*Teriyaki Sauce*—Substitute with ⅓ cup soy, 2 tsps garlic salt, 2 tsps sugar and ¼ cup water mixed.

HERBAMARE—This is a Swiss natural seasoning that is readily available in most health stores or in the health section of some supermarkets. It is very tasty and does not contain MSG. If possible, use it whenever you can—on vegetables, fish, chicken etc.

LAWRY'S ORIGINAL SEASONING SALT—This is readily available in most supermarkets worldwide. It is quite strong so use it sparingly, but it does not contain MSG. I find it particularly tasty on chicken and meat dishes.

MUSTARDS—I use Colman's mustards quite a lot. Their coarse grain mustard, Dijon etc., is delicious. I have used the Honey Mustard in some recipes. If you need to substitute with another mustard, then use the Colmans Coarse Grain Mustard powder dissolved with some mayonnaise and some honey to dilute it.

PUFF PASTRY—I use the "TODAY" brand, which is readily available in most supermarkets, but obviously any good quality puff pastry is acceptable.

STOCKS—Particularly in the soup section I have explained my use of the stock powders. I am a Knorr stock user. I don't believe that today's busy housewife has time to make her own stocks, so she will make use of what is available. Some stocks are stronger than others. Knorr is much more concentrated than Telma. In each recipe I have specified the exact amount to use. If however, you find it not strong enough or alternatively too strong, then add more stock or dilute with extra water if necessary. Stock powders are used exactly the same as cubes—2 tsps of powder to 1 cup of boiling water. I do, however, suggest that if you are kosher and can obtain the Telma chicken cubes which are marked Parev, these are a much better substitute than the vegetable cubes because they don't contain potato which thickens your stocks too much.

FETA CHEESE—In South Africa we have access to some wonderful local feta, which is made with herbs and black pepper. If this is not available in your country, then plain feta will be suitable but add some additional black pepper or dry mixed herbs where necessary to add the extra flavor.

NONDAIRY CREAMER—I have been using Rich's cream (sweetened) for ice creams wherever possible. It gives your ice cream a unique richness. If unavailable, use Instawhip or Orly Whip in the same quantities.

We also have access to Rich's Whip Kream (base), which when diluted with water can be a nondairy (parev) milk used to make white sauce etc. It can also be heated without separating. If you can obtain this for cooking purposes, it is a bonus for kosher or lactose intolerant people.

OLIVE OIL—I find the Italian olive oils the nicest because they are not too strong in flavor. I use light olive oil in all salad dressings. For cooking, a slightly darker olive oil can be used. I rarely use very dark extra virgin oils.

GARLIC—I find chopping fresh garlic quite irritating, so I use bottled minced garlic for all recipes where I have mentioned garlic. If however, you are using fresh garlic, substitute 1 clove for each ½ tsp minced bottled garlic.

YEAST—I always use Instant Dry Yeast. It is essential that you buy "Instant" yeast, as all others will not rise the same way. I find that buying fresh yeast is unnecessary if you know how to use instant. The greatest advantage of using instant yeast is that it does not have to proof (bubble). You simply mix in the dry ingredients, add moist ingredients, knead well and allow dough to rise.

SWEET POTATOES—Also known as "yams" in other countries.

EGGPLANT—Also known as "brinjals" in other countries.

PORCINI MUSHROOMS—These are not available all year-round as they are quite seasonal and very expensive when purchased fresh. They are very rich in flavor and do not have a high water content. When not in season, they are available dry. They may be kept in the freezer for as long as necessary. To reconstitute them, soak the mushrooms in enough boiling water to cover them for about 20 minutes until they are soft. The liquid retains a lot of flavor, so use it to make up the liquid quantity in the recipe.

NONSTICK COOKING SPRAY—I use this spray on roasting or baking sheets as it makes them easier to clean. I also spray my baking tins with nonstick cooking spray and then flour them very well. I do this in order to avoid using butter or margarine. However, if you are against using the spray for health reasons, there is no reason why you cannot butter and flour your tin.

CARAMELIZED NUTS—Ready-made caramelized nuts are available in supermarkets everywhere. Should you not be able to buy them, use the following guideline to make your own:

7 oz (200g) pecans, almonds, cashews, 1½ cups (175ml) sugar, 4 Tbs (60ml) water.

Bring the sugar and water to a boil in a heavy-bottomed pot. Allow to boil until sugar crystallises, melts and re-crystallizes. It will then start to brown on the bottom. Shake pot gently. Do not stir at all during this time. Only when it starts to brown can you stir it a little. Stir in the nuts to coat them. Turn them out onto a sprayed baking sheet. Allow to cool until set. Break up and chop accordingly.

CILANTRO OIL—Blanch 30g (1 OZ) fresh cilantro in boiling water for 1 min. Drain. Place in food processor with 2 tsps (10ml) salt & 2 Tbs (30ml) white wine vinegar. Process. Pour ¾ cup (175ml) olive oil down feed tube. Keep refrigerated in a bottle for up to 2 weeks. Bring to room temperature before using.

## PANTRY ESSENTIALS

| | |
|---|---|
| OILS | Olive oil, sunflower oil. |
| VINEGARS | Red wine, white wine, balsamic, rice vinegar. |
| PASTAS | Spaghetti, fettucine, capellini, angel-hair, penne, lasagne sheets. |
| BAKING NEEDS | White flour, self-raising flour, baking powder, sugar, icing sugar, finely granulated white sugar, soft brown sugar, vanilla extract, cocoa, dark chocolate, chocolate chips, cream of tartar, bicarbonate of soda, baking paper, syrup. |
| NUTS AND SEEDS | Pecans, walnuts, sesame seeds, almonds. |
| CANNED GOODS | Whole peeled tomatoes, tomato puree, tomato paste, asparagus cuts, asparagus spears, artichokes, tuna, salmon, anchovies, soups - tomato, pea, sweetcorn. Apricot jam, peach slices, strawberry jam, canned lychees. |
| DRIED GOODS | Long grain rice, Wild rice, Brown rice, Jasmine rice. |
| HERBS & SPICES | Salt, black peppercorns, white pepper, cayenne pepper, chili powder, curry powder, bay leaves, paprika, cinnamon, ginger, nutmeg, garlic salt, onion salt, chicken seasoning, oregano, sweet basil, thyme, rosemary, mixed herbs, Colmans dry mustard powder, chicken stock cubes, beef stock cubes, Herbamare, Lawry's original seasoning salt. |
| LIQUORS | Medium sherry, white wine, red wine, brandy, White Cinzano. |
| OTHERS | Tomato sauce, soy sauce, Worcestershire sauce, chutney, Dijon mustard, coarse grain mustard. |

## KITCHEN ESSENTIALS

| | |
|---|---|
| 3 | Frying pans |
| 2 | Small Pots |
| 1 | Medium Pot |
| 1 | Large Pot |
| 2 | Covered Casseroles |
| 2 | Roasting Pans |
| 1 | Springform tin—10 inch (26 cm) |
| 1 | Quiche tin |
| 2 | Baking sheets |
| 1 | Loaf tin |
| 1 | Steamer |
| 1 | Colander |
| 3 | Stainless Steel mixing bowls |
| 1 | Metal Lifter |
| 1 | Can Opener |
| 1 | Egg lifter |
| 2 | Wire Whisks |
| 3 | Wooden Spoons |
| 2 | Rubber spatulas |
| 2 | Ladles |
| 1 | Large slotted kitchen spoon |
| 1 | Large kitchen spoon |
| 1 | Long-handled kitchen fork |
| 1 | Metal Tongs |
| 1 | Kitchen scissors |
| 1 | 2-cup glass measuring cup |
| 1 | Set measuring spoons |
| 1 | Pastry bag with two tips |
| 2 | Pastry brushes |
| 1 | Rolling pin |
| 2 | Chopping boards |
| 1 | Vegetable Peeler |
| 2 | Strainers—1 large, 1 small |
| 4 | Knives—1 Paring, 1 boning, 1 slicing, 1 chef's knife |
| 1 | Sharpening tool for knives |
| 1 | Pepper mill |
| 1 | Timer |
| 1 | Scale |
| 1 | Grater |
| 1 | Food processor |
| 1 | Blender |
| 1 | Electric hand mixmaster and/or 1 Mixmaster |
| 1 | Spaghetti measure |
| 1 | Muffin tin |
| 2 | Round layer tins |
| 1 | Egg Slicer |
| 1 | Baster |
| 1 | Oven Gloves |
| 1 | Mallet |

# INDEX

# INDEX

## A

## B

## C

## D

## E

## F

## G

## H